EQUUS CABALLUS

*On horses
and handling*

EQUUS CABALLUS

On horses and handling

JAN MAY

Throughout this book specific words are used in describing certain horse handling procedures. A helpful glossary of terms is located at the rear of this book to explain these terms in detail.

British Library Cataloguing-in-Publication Data.
A catalogue record for this book is available from the British Library.

ISBN 0.85131.616.6

© J.A. Allen & Co. Ltd, 1995.

Published in Great Britain in 1995 by
J.A. Allen & Company Limited,
1 Lower Grosvenor Place, Buckingham Palace Road,
London, SW1W OEL

Typeset in Australia by LinkLetters, Perth, Western Australia.
Printed in Hong Kong by Dah Hua Printing Press Co. Ltd.

Designed by Barry May

FOREWORD

I have had the notion of writing a book on horse handling for many years because, as I went about my work, it became apparent that many people were dangerously ignorant of what makes and maintains obedience and good manners in a horse. Predictably, when handling horses, people often try to outsmart their charges with human thinking, but approaching the problem as it is seen through the eyes of the horse eventually removes the guesswork completely.

Horses *are* what we make them.

They are incapable of making a logical decision as we know it; they simply react to their surroundings. This book is, therefore, written ultimately for the benefit of the horse by giving the reader an insight to those unique qualities that make up the horse's character, a character that is essentially forgiving.

JAN MAY

CONTENTS

PART ONE

The Language of the Horse

In this section, we explore the essential character of the horse which has resulted from the imprint of 70 million years of evolution, and the myriad signals that his behaviour can yield, allowing us to map his responses both in and beyond the world of people.

1 THE HORSE, NATURALLY

Through evolution, he has been gifted with highly developed senses of sight, smell and hearing, and, being essentially timid, uses another great gift, that of speed, to distance himself from predators, man and beast.

2 READING THE HORSE

By studying the horse's conformation, that is the way in which the body is shaped, and to 'read' him as he talks to us through his body movements, is to see the full language of the horse.

3 FEARS AND OTHER MOTIVATORS

Fear is by far the greatest component in the emotional make-up of the horse and its correct use in motivating a horse to action, therefore, ultimately dictates success or failure at the hands of the trainer.

1. The horse, naturally

In his natural environment, the horse survives by instinct. Through evolution, he has been gifted with highly developed senses of sight, smell and hearing and, being essentially timid, uses another great gift, that of speed, to distance himself from predators both human and animal. He has an uncommon capacity for endurance, coupled with exceptional surefootedness, and, because of his timidity, is most confident in open places.

COLOUR BLIND

The horse is colour blind and, compared to a human, has a distinctly different view of the world. His eye measures the intensity of colour as light or dark shades of grey, but is unable to distinguish red from green. What we can see as a green paddock, he will smell as 'green', for, while his eyes do not detect colour, his other senses more than compensate by delivering a feast of information about his surroundings.

AN ASTONISHING DEPTH OF FIELD

His eye is quite different to that of a human. In photographic terms, one would say that its depth of field is truly astonishing. While viewing you at one metre's distance, the horse can simultaneously focus beyond you to scan the horizon, which he does with great accuracy. Moreover, his natural vision is truly unique – adjusting focus is achieved simply by head movement. (People suffering from acute long or short sightedness also do this to obtain clear focus.) In the human eye the retina is evenly curved, which means that all parts of it are at the same distance from the lens at the front of the eye. However, the horse's retina is constructed differently, forming an irregular curve that is nearer the lens in the lower half of the eye and more distant in the upper half. It is this peculiarity which gives the horse's vision such a notable advantage. For example, while grazing, the horse is not only able to see the grass but also the horizon and almost everything that surrounds him.

MONOCULAR VISION

The horse makes considerable use of yet another gift, that of monocular vision, i.e. the ability to use each eye independently. Because his eyes are placed on the side of his head, he has the ability to take in two different images simultaneously. In fact, except for a small block to vision caused by his own body, he is able to see throughout almost 360 degrees. This view is a wide, flat panorama, much like a very wide movie screen with sharp images and foreground and horizon detail, but, because of his inability to distinguish colour in this world, the scene is defined only in terms of light and dark tones and shapes.

When the horse's attention is dominated by his alarm system, he shifts from monocular vision to binocular vision, i.e. the ability to focus both eyes forwards towards one object. This achieves a vastly increased perception of depth but at some cost, for it eliminates his side and rear vision. This forward-vision mode is maintained for a short time only, enabling the horse to appraise the object in focus quickly as friend or foe. Interestingly, when both eyes are focused forwards, so too are the ears, providing a back-up of sound data on which to base his decision to run or stay.

PECKING ORDER

By nature the horse is a herd animal and this strong pull in his character invariably prompts him to join a group where a hierarchy, or pecking

Until some time after the installation of the Olympian Games, the use of the horse was confined to war and the chase. These games were held every four years and are said to have commenced about 774 BC. The birth of horse racing began in approximately 680 BC in the Olympic arena. The races were first ridden over a distance of 6.5 km (4 miles). In the 25th Olympiad, the chariot was introduced and became an instrument to test the horses' speed and endurance.

The earliest recorded mention of a horse can be found in the Old Testament, Genesis 36, where it was said to exist in the wilderness of Idomea (North West Africa), at the beginning of the sixteenth century BC.

order, exists. This hierarchy fulfils the essential needs for protection of each individual horse, giving the herd its order, strength and leadership.

Although the leader is generally a stallion, this role can, at times, be taken over by a mature mare. The trappings of leadership are evident, the leader being allowed the tastiest grazing and to drink first at a waterhole. These privileges also exact payment, however, for it is on the leader that the duty of full alertness falls, it is his or her responsibility to forewarn the herd of any danger. The leader establishes his or her superior strength by demonstrations of nipping and kicking at the lower members of the herd's hierarchy.

ON FULL ALERT

The natural timidity of the horse always leaves a small corner of his senses on full alert, so that he can respond to virtually all unfamiliar situations instantly. A warning signal can be anything that does not compute visually as safe, such as loud noises, strange or unknown smells and even signals beyond the range of human senses. Climatic changes, although too subtle for human senses, will often coax him on to new grazing grounds.

There is yet another side to the horse which begs mention at this point. Having recognised his benign attributes, it is also well to remember that, denied flight into open ground, he will, in fear, resort to biting savagely and his kick has been known to kill. In appreciating the character traits that his long evolution has bestowed on *Equus Caballus*, we can also understand the reasons for his reactions when confined for our purposes. In proceeding to eliminate all of these natural, but somewhat alarm-sensitive senses that make up the horse's character, a sensitive handler seeks to put him in what is best expressed as 'non-threatening mode'.

SUPERIOR MEMORY

To understand the horse thoroughly as a prerequisite to handling, one must realise that his brain has no capacity *whatsoever* for reasoning. He cannot, nor will he ever, have the ability for considered thought. His brain is merely a mechanism for guiding him from minute to minute through his world. His waking brain functions solely according to the law of stimulus and response, causing him to react appropriately to avoid danger or simply to seek the next blade of grass. So, when a horse gallops off, his mind has registered threat and when he begins to eat, it is because his mind has registered this as a pleasant experience worth repeating. Neither act was a consideration, only a reaction.

The horse has *much feeling* but *little understanding*. This means that he is guided by instinct and that rational thought plays very little part in his actions. A horse is, therefore, less intelligent than a dog, although his memory is far superior.

FLIGHT RESPONSES

When we transport these truths into the working arena, our success depends on the horse receiving signals that do not spark responses of fear or flight. The wild horse is fundamentally no different to any other creature in the animal kingdom in that he only has the ability to respond immediately to a current stimulus. He cannot foretell what is likely to happen and has no capacity for measured thinking whatsoever.

The curb bit was invented by the Romans but both they and the Greeks were ignorant of the use of the stirrup. The use of the stirrup can be traced back to the Norman invasion of England and has been recorded on the eleventh century Bayeux Tapestry.

2. Reading the horse

By studying the horse's conformation, i.e. the way in which the body is shaped, and 'reading' him as he talks to us through his body movements, we can see the full language of the horse – the only way in which he can communicate his moods, feelings and reaction to us. It is a precise language that takes time to study and fully understand. As this skill develops in the trainer, so more subtle signs will be detected, interpreted and correctly understood. In much the same way as it takes time to achieve fluency in a new language, so, too, 'reading' your horse accurately will require persistent study and patience.

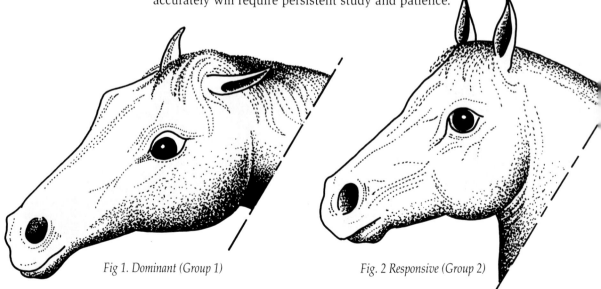

Fig 1. Dominant (Group 1)

Fig. 2 Responsive (Group 2)

Fig. 3 Indifferent (Group 3)

Well into the 1950s, the engine capacity of a passenger car was still being rated as equal to the pulling power of a set number of horses (e.g. a 10 horse power saloon).

DOMINANT, RESPONSIVE OR INDIFFERENT

Horses, like humans, come in all shapes and sizes and, like humans, some horses are more adept at certain tasks than others. Some favour show jumping and disciplines requiring speed and agility, while others are better suited for long-distance competitions and still others make ideal childrens' mounts. All horses, however, have certain telltale characteristics that yield clues as to their suitability for certain purposes and, by careful observation, these will readily be discovered.

In horses collectively, there are three distinct hierarchical categories: group 1 (dominant), group 2 (responsive) and group 3 (indifferent) (Figs. 1, 2 and 3). As knowledge is acquired of these types, the ability to assess the character of an individual horse becomes much easier. This knowledge will then guide the best approach when handling a particular horse on the ground. Establishing up front which of these three categories a horse falls into is fundamental to successful handling at a later date, as this information will provide the bedrock on which to base many other judgements about the horse.

SIGNAL CLUSTERS

Other judgements amount to reading and interpreting the many signals given out by various parts of the horse's body and the way in which he uses them. This chapter is concerned with these finer points. However, while the following will reveal to you the components of the horse's basic character through reading his body, it is important to assess the overall impression you receive as individual details of conformation can give a somewhat false impression when interpreted in isolation. Put another way, the three categories of horse body language – conformation, signals and movements – need to be read as clusters of signals in order to receive an accurate overall impression.

Isolated details of conformation can provide only a basic insight into the main temperament of the horse. For example, observing the horse's head offers many conformation clues but this also involves the ears, forehead, eyes, nose, mouth and lips, all of which can be read as a cluster, giving strong indicators of his real personality and temperament. We hope the following will help in building up a catalogue of signs that the horse's body offers as clues to his personality and as to how he will behave or perform.

EYES

The shape, size and position of the eye and how it is set on the head vary considerably from horse to horse and, when observed under the cluster rule, should enable you to make a fairly accurate decision as to his disposition. For example, a large, clear, 'soft' eye, set out towards the side of the head, indicates a tractable, reliable type that is probably in the middle bracket or group 2 (responsive) of the hierarchy.

This softness is found in the deep colour of the eye and is reminiscent of peering into a deep well, offering a sense of calmness (Fig. 4). However, this type of eye coupled with a marked bright activity (Fig. 2) will, instead, put him in the top group 1 (dominant) bracket. His eyes will be alert to his surroundings but he will quickly turn his attention back to his handler when requested. An alert eye coupled with body signals that show tension, such as head held high, nostrils open wide seeking scents, and feet firmly and securely in touch with the ground, gives signals that he will, at a moment's notice, respond to the flight stimulus should the situation warrant it.

In the type of horse referred to as the White Horse (Cremello), an eye known as a 'fish eye' is often seen. This is distinctive by its blue colour

'If the throat is sore, an embrocation of equal parts of oil, turpentine, tincture of cantharides (powder from crushed spanish fly) and harts horn (ammonia, formerly distilled from deer horn), may be rubbed in night and morning.'
THE HORSE IN THE STABLE AND FIELD, J.H. WALSH (1883)

Fig. 4 Soft calm eye

Fig. 5 Nervous, unpredictable temperament

and is not to be considered a fault in this particular type. When viewing the eye, you should also take into consideration the amount of white that is visible around it (Fig. 5). As long as it is minimal, and seen mostly when the horse is looking behind it or to the side without head movement, it is quite acceptable. Indeed, the white around the eye can be seen clearly in certain breeds such as the Appaloosa and is, in fact, a requirement in that breed's definition, so it should not be interpreted as a defect.

'PIGGY'-EYED

The 'piggy'-eyed horse is characterised by small, unfriendly eyes, usually set towards the front of the face. This feature also indicates an unpredictable animal. Because of the size and positioning of this type of eye, the horse is sometimes found to be suffering from defective vision, making him unsuitable for any riding activity. When using his eyesight, this horse will display traits of insecurity, continually moving his head to compensate for his inadequate vision. His body will display tension – his muscles tightening – and he will move his body from side to side as he tries desperately to focus on the unfamiliar scene before him.

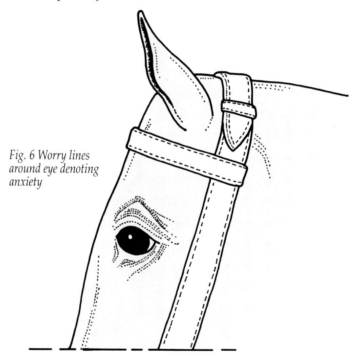

Fig. 6 Worry lines around eye denoting anxiety

EYELIDS AND WORRY LINES

The eyelids should be thin, allowing the eyeball to move freely with few or no worry lines seen above the eye (Fig. 6). If these lines are constantly present, this could well indicate that the horse is either anxious or has a health problem. When asked to face an unknown situation, horses can show such worry lines above the eyes but, once the horse has sensed no threat they should readily disappear.

The forehead should be wide and flat, with little or no bulge between the eyes. When present, a bulge may indicate a sullen creature lacking good qualities. It is often found hand in hand with small eyes and, although showing alertness, the horse's attention is likely to wander as his focus is, in fact, interrupted by this conformation fault, giving him a somewhat false impression of the world around him.

EARS

Because the eyes and ears of a horse work together, small, active ears, continually flicking back and forth or focused in the same direction as the eye, will indicate a horse of dominant nature (Fig. 1). It is important that this horse be handled in a confident manner, ensuring that the trainer achieves the role of leader in the partnership.

A large, soft eye, coupled with big floppy ears which are generally set close together, can very often indicate a stubborn or sullen animal from group 3 (indifferent), even more so if the ears flop to the side in a disinterested fashion (Fig. 7). It can often be noted that the eye, too, has a definitely disinterested look, only showing a marked change in appearance when the horse is confronted with an unfamiliar situation.

Unlike a group 1 (dominant) horse, a group 3 type lacks the 'sparkle' of a leader and, after viewing the situation, reverts quickly to the disinterested mode. His body, too, will lack the attentiveness of a group 1 horse, the muscles will remain relaxed and he may shift his weight from one hind leg to the other. His head will be raised a little, the big ears routinely collecting sound-based information, but everything except grazing is too much effort and he will show little response.

Not surprisingly, these group 3 character traits suggest that this horse is likely to show an unwillingness to co-operate and will need careful

'Shouldering' is understood as the attempt to crush the leg of a rider against a wall, which ill-tempered horses are fond of doing. It is easily avoided by pulling the horse's head towards the wall instead of from it.
THE HORSE IN THE STABLE AND FIELD, J.H. WALSH (1883)

Fig. 7 Ears flopped to side
denoting disinterest or stubborness

handling. In general, this stubborn type is also an unpredictable animal,
prone to sudden and erratic behaviour.

MOUTH AND LIPS

The mouth, too, can reveal many clues. A relaxed, closed mouth and lips
usually indicate a horse that will willingly accept any request from the
handler. If he has small eyes and/or large floppy ears, however, he is
most likely to show initial resistance. For example, a foal that has been
asked to do a new task and has not understood it completely may 'pout'
his upper lip (much like a child when unhappy or insecure) but, having
then understood and having been rewarded, he will take a deep breath
and sigh, chew his lips and relax in the mouth.

NOSE

Apart from the unfortunate aesthetics of the shape, a Roman nose is quite
acceptable and generally suggests a predictable and trustworthy disposition in a horse. Some years ago I owned a mare with the ugliest head
imaginable. She had a big head, big nose and a bulge between the eyes
but a very kind eye. She never put a foot wrong, could be trusted
implicitly and was eventually sold on to a novice rider who still owns her
to this day.

TAIL

The actions of the tail also convey many useful messages to the alert student of horse language. Firstly, it should always hang naturally, following the line of the spine (Fig. 8). If you observe a horse in a paddock, whether on his own or within a group, when startled he will trot off with a definite spring in his feet (much like an antelope when pursued by a lion). At the same time, his tail will be raised high above his back, signalling to the other horses his 'flight' response. Generally, only one or two horses within the group will show this group 1 trait. The others will quickly respond by raising their heads from grazing and then galloping off.

In breeds such as the Arab, the tail is expected to be carried at a slightly higher angle because of the unique conformation of this breed and it should not be considered a fault. When handling the dock, it should feel heavy and relaxed in the hand, enabling you to swing it gently from side to side.

The tail appears to be intended chiefly to protect the body from insects but it also serves, to some extent, as an aid in balancing the body when moving rapidly in any new direction. It is composed of between 15 and 18 bones.

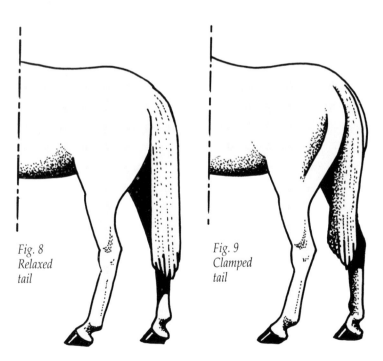

Fig. 8
Relaxed
tail

Fig. 9
Clamped
tail

CLAMPING THE TAIL

A horse of a nervous disposition will tend to 'clamp' his tail tightly to his hindquarters (Fig. 9). This clamping of the tail also causes the main muscles in the rump to become tense. If it is at all possible to touch the horse at such times, the rump will feel like a tight drum and a number of lines on the skin's surface may accompany this tightness. If, at the same time as clamping his tail, the horse also shifts his weight on to his hindquarters, dropping them slightly, there is a strong possibility that he will run forwards or to the side, away from your hand. Almost all horses will tend to show this trait when faced with a 'trapped' situation, e.g. when being put in a yard or box for the first time or in any environment that is unfamiliar to him. On hearing or smelling the unfamiliar, he will rush forward, clamping his tail and feeling vulnerable and insecure but, once reassured, the tail will loosen and relax.

TAIL SWISHING

Continual and fierce swishing of the tail can also indicate that he is nervous and uncertain (or, perhaps, that you are too rough in grooming). At times, a horse can betray tension caused by anticipation (observed mostly with group 1 and, sometimes, group 2 types). This swishing of the tail can be seen, for example, at the beginning of a race as the horse anticipates the gallop, or when sensing that his rider is nervous and excited prior to hunting or competition riding.

A horse that is tied up and flicks his tail at you at the same time as he folds his ears back when you are passing him, is telling you to keep out of his space. (This habit should never be tolerated as it leads to more serious vices such as biting and kicking.) He will twist his head to focus attention on what is behind him as he raises his leg in preparation to kick, at the same time dropping his weight on to his hindquarters and leaning back on the rope as far as possible. This is often overlooked as a harmless habit when approaching a horse in a yard or box before he has had his first face-up lesson (this is explained in detail in Part Two 'Equipment and how to use it').

BEHAVIOUR REVEALED

These signs are there for us to read and interpret. They are a guide to the complex language that the horse has to offer as a means of communicating with us. The horse has an immense capacity to learn but it is the way in which he has already been taught that is revealed in his behaviour. As experience is gained, more subtle signs and clusters will be observed.

About the year 1835, horses were imported from Great Britain to Australia, where they adapted well to the environment and climate and were put to use in agriculture, racing and transportation. Before this time, inferior types were imported from India but were found wanting in quality and stamina. Cross breeding with the English Thoroughbred produced a horse with exceptional speed, strength and endurance.

3. Fear and other motivators

Fear is by far the most dominant component in the emotional make up of the horse and its use by the trainer in motivating a horse to action will dictate success or failure. Ultimately, it is true to say that, from the very earliest recorded relationships between trainer and horse, the latter has continued to fare badly from the experience. Throughout the last 25 centuries at least, and almost certainly before that, man has employed a variety of cruel handling methods in his endeavour to force the humble horse to comply with the ambitions of his owner.

A CAUTIONARY NOTE

It was, and still is in some quarters, routine practice for sharp and severe bits, coupled with harsh whippings, to be used as part of the training procedure. Now, as in the past, such mind bending ignorance serves only to inflict severe pain for paltry result. It is well to remember that no horse ever yielded his maximum potential in response to pain and abuse. If the foregoing seems somewhat pointed, it is because the basic tenets of this book are dedicated to reducing fear to a minimum in the educated horse's daily programme. Any cruel treatment is, therefore, contrary to this book's purpose and direction in generating trust in the horse's perception of the humans around him.

NOT SMARTER, JUST DIFFERENT

In stark contrast to the desired result, a bad handler unwittingly creates a 'problem' animal. A downward spiral will be produced. As fear is increased in pursuit of results when training incorrectly, so the quality of the resulting training diminishes, eventually to a point where the horse is of no use. Cruel treatment causes a horse to rebel and it is in this way that such unwelcome vices as rearing, bolting and biting are generated. It is no coincidence that a rough and impatient rider invariably exhibits the same shortcomings in their handling of the horse during groundwork. A surprising number of people who have regular contact with horses abuse their charges, yet when these incorrect handling activities deliver the wrong result, the handler sees only a horse that has failed. When we consider that the horse *cannot* think, as we understand thinking, then we begin to appreciate that we are not necessarily smarter than the horse, just different.

THE 'THINKING' HORSEMAN

All coins have two sides as they say and, on the good side, history shows ample proof of 'thinking' horsemen, people who have applied kindness and skill to achieve a superior and lasting result. The 'thinking' horse handler of the past first set about creating a mutual trust between man and horse. The result was a light, attentive and, most importantly, unfrightened animal, responsive and predictable both under saddle and in hand. The 'thinking' trainer today still achieves much the same in standards of training excellence by applying consistency and accuracy in their approach to handling horses. There is nothing casual or vague about their manner when around horses. They display an alertness and confidence born of knowing that they will reach their stated goal. This involves kindness, too, and these skills always produce the same result – an obedient horse displaying a willingness to oblige. Why does this work? It works because the one thing a horse wants more than anything else is to be free of fear, therefore he constantly seeks a non-threatening situation and a good trainer uses this fact to make progress.

Having approached a young or unhandled horse, remember to walk away before he moves away from you.

17

'*M*any farmers break their colts in by putting them to plough between two other horses, but the pull at this work is too dead for well bred colts, and many jibbers are produced in this way. A jibber being a horse having a habitual reluctance to move forward on command.'
THE HORSE IN THE STABLE AND FIELD, J.H. WALSH (1883)

BIRTH OF A PROBLEM

Insecurity in any horse brings about bad habits but it is important to realise that the horse has absolutely no idea that he has formed either good or bad habits. A horse is, however, quickly labelled 'bad' or 'rogue' because of habits that have been formed, in the main, through incorrect or inadequate handling during earlier times. Some trainers are, perhaps, too quick to use the whip in seeking solutions to problems and the resulting apprehension manifested by the horse is there for the balance of his life. He lives in constant fear and this stress eventually produces a 'problem' horse. The horse is then passed from owner to owner, the habit becoming progressively worse as he is further abused in a vain attempt to correct the problem.

FROM BIRTH TO VICE

This sad train of events rarely has a happy ending. Many fine horses have been declared useless and subsequently shot as a result of a history of bad handling.

It is not an exaggeration to say that problems in horses result, in the main, from problems in the people who handle those horses. However, there is another side to this, which involves the overly sensitive or emotional horse owner, a person who is generally too inexperienced to nip an emerging 'problem' in the bud before it develops into a more serious and undesirable vice. Given time, such people go a long way towards killing the horse by applying their own particular version of kindness and, on occasions, can get severely injured themselves. A likely scenario is when the horse, having been shown no boundaries of correct conduct, is allowed to indulge (with the begrudging consent of the owner) in biting, kicking and rearing. Problems like this rapidly develop into full-blown vices, difficult to deal with and dangerous in the extreme. Such a horse, eventually labelled as having 'vices', would probably have become a very useful animal in more experienced hands for, as is often stated, there are no problem horses, only problem owners.

THE NATURE OF FEAR AND OF TRUST

The purpose of this chapter is to explain the nature of fear in the horse. Because fear is central to his emotional responses, our purpose thus far has been to explain that fear, whether intentionally stimulated or otherwise in a handled horse, is, in truth, diametrically opposed to the ambitions of the trainer. When fear is provoked in a horse during handling or training, its capacity to learn becomes significantly reduced and, in severe cases involving cruelty, can even be permanently retarded.

In attempting to train or re-educate a horse, therefore, it is vitally important that a bond of confidence is created between the horse and yourself because, without confidence, the horse will not respond willingly. He may very well perform the tasks set him but these will be

'To achieve prompt obedience, the same signal and word used in teaching the task must be repeated exactly, with the same tone and pitch in the voice, thus avoiding confusion in messages relayed to him.'
JAN MAY

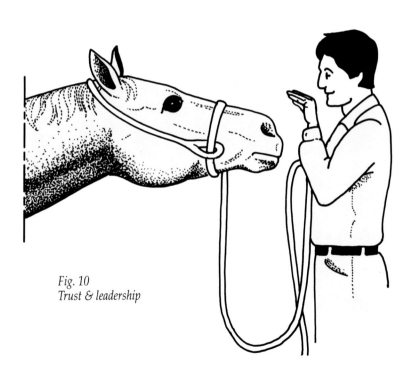

Fig. 10
Trust & leadership

achieved with a large degree of apprehension. When he trusts you, however, because he has come to know that you will not put him at risk, he will then follow you anywhere, doing anything that you ask of him. By trust or confidence, therefore, we mean that the horse gives in willingly to the handler's requests, without any trace of fear. This state can be described as total subservience, in that the horse gladly performs any task requested of him. Achievement of this trust comes about through the physical actions and emotional equilibrium of the handler, conveying to the horse their absolute confidence (Fig. 10). You cannot fake this; the horse will know.

THE SCENT OF ADRENALIN

Your attitude, thoughts, reactions and even your perception of him are all important clues to the horse's senses in assessing you. He senses fear and uncertain thoughts and is extremely sensitive to the feel and touch of humans. When a human is nervous or uncertain, their heart beats faster and this stimulates the flow of adrenalin through the veins. Adrenalin is an organic chemical which has the effect of causing an increase in blood pressure, which, in turn, increases the heart rate. Because it is associated with alarm, the horse 'reads' the odour of adrenalin as fear and so reacts, in turn, as if alarmed. Adrenalin is, in fact, nature's original early-warning system. Through his acute sense of smell, the horse has the ability to recognise the odour of adrenalin as it excretes through your skin when you become anxious, angry, uncertain or impatient. It is therefore very important to cheat this chemical signal by maintaining a neutral attitude in your movements and thinking and developing a quiet and positive feeling of progress. The horse's strongest instinct is always to get away from the unfamiliar and detecting fear or uncertainty in the handler is most likely to cause such a response. Once having assumed the role of dominant leader, you must allow the horse to feel totally secure with you.

THE DOMINANT LEADER

Because of the horse's nature, he is always capable of, and amenable to, being dominated by a leader once that role has been established by another. As handlers, therefore, we have to assume the role of leader or dominant partner, but without showing any aggression. There must be positiveness in all that we do and an absence of any personal doubt when in the horse's company. Once achieved, this attitude will be the most effective way to stay in control and to handle horses successfully.

SEVERAL MILLION YEARS OF EVOLUTION

The horse's need for leadership is well seated in his nature and stems from behaviour patterns spanning several million years of evolution as a herd animal, where leadership has been essential to group survival. Within the herd, a horse finds his natural place, which will be one that suits his particular disposition or temperament. All horses have similar instincts and reactions, but their levels of intelligence and strength, physical build and temperament vary enormously. Under certain circumstances, different horses respond in different ways (as you progress in handling a variety of types, you will gain the ability to 'read' this temperament). Their senses of hearing, sight and smell also vary considerably and this, too, has a definite bearing on the disposition of each individual horse. Some horses even have a defective sensory system, causing them to become stressed more rapidly than others because the signals they receive from their surroundings are incorrectly interpreted. The small-eyed horse, for example, cannot see as well as the horse with large eyes set well spaced on his head, therefore he feels less secure in any environment.

In his inherited pattern of behaviour, the horse displays a natural reaction to certain stimuli, and this, depending on his 'social' or 'hierarchical' behaviour pattern, will determine how he is to be handled. So how do these strong herd instincts affect handling?

A TEST FOR THE HANDLER

Any horse that you have to re-educate or handle (bearing in mind that, until this point, you have been an unknown entity), will put you through a series of tests to establish leadership. The outcome *must* prove you the

'The six year old mouth is the last upon which any great reliance can be placed, if it is desired to ascertain the age of the horse to a nicety, but by attentively studying both jaws, a near approximation to the truth may be arrived at.'
THE HORSE IN THE STABLE AND FIELD, J.H. WALSH (1883)

clear winner. In essence, these tests happen because the horse needs to know where he stands in any new relationship and, once established, this knowledge will effectively reduce his level of fear. If the horse has been the leader in his previous environment, he will naturally assume the same superiority with you and, initially, will take offence at being reduced in rank. However, once your dominance has been established in the partnership, he will happily relinquish the superior role to you, his handler.

THE FIRST ENCOUNTER

In the first handling session, the group 1 (dominant) type invariably strongly resists any idea of relinquishing his dominance and will require well-chosen and positive requests from the handler in order to effect good results. The group 2 (responsive) type will also display strong, dominating traits but lacks the unique leadership qualities of a group 1 horse, tending to withdraw from the handler when feeling insecure, unlike a group 1 horse, who shows assertiveness by standing his ground.

Finally, at the lowest end of the herd hierarchy, is the group 3 (indifferent) type. This horse has a 'couldn't care less, just let me eat' approach to life and, because of his disinterest in confronting the world around him (relying on the group 1 or group 2 horses in the herd to warn him of danger), he often shows a sullen and pig-headed character, akin to someone forced to wake up and pay attention. When faced with re-education, the group 3 type has been known to sit down on the job and flatly refuse to show any inclination to co-operate.

RIGHT HORSE, WRONG READING

Unfortunately, many people, even those who handle horses on a regular basis, have scant knowledge of these three primary horse types, which leads handlers and trainers alike into misreading the true nature of the horse. They assess the animal incorrectly, making wrong judgements over a course of handling or re-education. They may apply training at a speed that is too fast for the horse to understand, or may use force on a horse, unaware that he is a group 1 (dominant) type. The list of examples is endless but we trust the point has been made. The handler wrongly applies remedial treatment in an attempt to *correct* the uncorrectable. It is easy to see that great fear can be generated in a horse by handling that is inappropriate to his nature. Put simply, a group 3 (indifferent) horse cannot be whipped into becoming a group 1 (dominant) horse. A reasonable analogy is that if you wish to own a fast car, it is better not to buy a slow one because, despite all your efforts, it is still going to be a slow car. The 'thinking' handler recognises the kind of horse they are working with as they have made their observations well in advance and have assessed the animal's personality traits and, more importantly, his limits. The trainer then sets about reducing any fear that may be present, knowing that only then will they achieve much with ease.

READ THE SIGNS

You may have been fortunate enough in acquiring a very friendly and inquisitive horse but, before making the initial approach to the horse in the box or yard, you should exercise caution by observing his disposition and temperament, spending some time watching *him*, as he watches *you*. By noting his approach to his surroundings and you, it is possible to make an assessment of what he considers his status to be in the hierarchy of horses.

Sit on the fence and watch his responses. If he trots around the yard, stopping occasionally to focus on you while flaring his nostrils and, at times, demonstrating his dominance by a harmless ritual display of aggression, you can assume from these actions that he considers himself to be top dog (dominant). If you stepped into this unhandled horse's area or yard, he would be likely to turn his hindquarters abruptly to you and might even back up towards you, in preparation to kick. Alternatively, he could face you with his head high and a 'dare approach me' expression on his face. Because of his dominating character, this horse will prove a challenging animal to work with but, having then relinquished his superiority in accepting you as leader, he will submit willingly to any task

'If a domestic horse never broken in be suddenly saddled and mounted, the rider has greater difficulties to encounter, for the animal is not gifted by nature with all the propensities of the wild horse to reject man but, being better fed, he has greater strength to indulge in them.'
THE HORSE IN THE STABLE AND FIELD, J.H. WALSH (1883)

asked of him.

Alternatively, if the horse chose to retreat to the far side of the area or yard with both eyes focused on you, preferring to stand his ground, giving the onlooker a false impression of physical strength, he could be considered group 2 (responsive) in the hierarchy. A group 3 (indifferent) type would show all the classic characteristics of subservience. He would display a total acceptance of his surroundings by walking slowly around the area or yard, smelling the unfamiliar but not showing any anxiety traits, such as high blowing or trotting. His approach would be casual as this is his true personality.

EVERYTHING REMEMBERED, RIGHT OR WRONG

In the horse's mind to make the unfamiliar familiar is to reduce fear, so that he will then accept what is asked without stress. Horses cannot reason but have remarkable memories (much like a tape recording of past events). They remember everything, both right and wrong. However, you must realise that they do not *know* right from wrong. If a horse takes a fall or slips while backing out of a trailer or float, from that moment on this will be embedded in his memory as an uncomfortable experience. He lacks the ability to think, 'Oh, I must be careful the next time I come out of the trailer because I slipped last time'. On coming out of the trailer or float a second time, his reaction will be to come out very fast as he has learnt from the previous experience that something unpleasant is about to happen.

The scenario might run something like this. As the tailgate is lowered, the horse displays tension, like a coiled spring waiting for release. His head goes up and, with ears and eyes turned back, he resists backing out because he is waiting for trouble. With experience, it eventually becomes possible to locate the cause of such problems in the animal's past. The problem can then be split up into sequential tasks, starting with the original wrong move. Stamped somewhere in his memory is a reactive response to this unpleasant experience and we need to locate this first before overriding it through re-education with modified behaviour.

THE HORSE'S ESCAPE ROUTE

As a herd animal, the horse has always searched for escape routes when faced with a stressful situation. If he has learnt to depend on a handler for direction, a situation can arise whereby he feels insecure about refusing what has been requested. In this case, if the fear on both sides is *not* equal he will look for the lesser fear. For example, if he has been asked to walk past a loud noise and he is worried but has confidence in the trainer, he may hesitate but still complete the task. However, if his fear of the noise is *greater* and confidence in the trainer *less,* he will simply refuse to obey. The important point here is that should these two considerations of trainer and noise become equal sources of fear for the horse, it is then that he seeks an escape route. He has no control over this reaction because he has no capacity for thought or reason.

FEAR CONFIRMED

Think of your horse's memory as a cassette tape loaded with thousands of previous experiences. Every waking minute of his life is spent in responding to these messages. It is important to remember that when the horse is troubled by a situation and is displaying the potential to flee through fear, stroking and, at times, talking to your horse actually reinforce in his mind that there really is something to be frightened of. In contrast, if the handler adopts a neutral attitude, then the horse may well ignore the alarming situation. Nine times out of ten, he will simply be reacting to your well-intentioned 'patting and reassuring'.

Emotion and affection are two different things for a horse. His emotion is nervousness without thought, a natural mechanism that drives his reactions. Becoming angry and losing your patience simply serves to heighten this nervous emotion, keeping it active in him. In contrast, if you are relaxed, quiet and calm, he will be the same.

THE WORST RESPONSE OF ALL

Hitting a horse at any time is a wrong move but doubly so when he is frightened, when abuse will merely intensify his fear. As a result of pressure accumulated through demands to complete a task, the horse will

In excellent bas-reliefs found in the ruins of Nineveh and dating from 3000-2000 BC, an Egyptian horse is shown as having a large and coarse head, high chest and a heavy, lumbering body not dissimilar to the Flemish horse of the nineteenth century.

reach a point where he refuses because the pressure has now become equal to his fear of the task. At this point, the habit of rearing or bolting begins to form as a response. Thus we begin to see that all of the horse's escape mechanisms are triggered through a stressful situation involving the generation of fear. This problem requires careful retraining in order to overcome and reprogramme the base fear. This is done by attempting to lodge a new response in the horse's memory, which overrides the old, fearful one. It is, however, at times impossible to locate the cause of these fears, so that the horse then becomes an unknown quantity and a danger to be near. Fortunately, such instances are the exception to the rule, as the vast majority of horses displaying problems of one kind or another can successfully be re-educated using thought, kindness, patience and confidence. A candid view of horse ownership will reveal that it takes the same amount of time and money to maintain a good horse as it does a bad, dangerous and unpredictable one.

THE WAR BRIDLE

Central to the training techniques described in this book is the use of the war bridle, a single length of rope which when fashioned to fit the horse's head, allows total control by the handler. Despite its somewhat sinister name, the war bridle is a gentle but remarkably effective form of training aid. When used correctly it can achieve excellent and permanent results, while avoiding the use of restraints usually associated with conventional training and schooling.

It is not possible to date when the first war bridle was employed as a training aid, but it was certainly used as a simple form of bridle by the American Indians and was probably used by them as a form of training aid when breaking horses to ride. Somewhat later, a type of war bridle is described in the book *The Classic Encyclopedia of the Horse* by Dennis Magner (1887).

It is no exaggeration to say that the war bridle is by far the best form of training aid yet devised as it achieves an instant and painless response from the horse. For this reason it is an aid that requires sensitive use by the handler, ensuring that the message conveyed is clearly understood, so that the horse remains calm and free from anxiety and fear. The war bridle is a deceptively simple piece of equipment but when applied in the right way, the handler achieves total control over the horse's every movement.

PART TWO

Hands-on Experience

With the benefit of our knowledge of the horse's true nature, as revealed in Part One, we now view, in some detail, equipment and how to use it in the essential lessons that provide sound understanding between horse and handler.

4 EQUIPMENT AND HOW TO USE IT

Through the effective use of the war bridle, total control over a horse can be achieved in groundwork, and it therefore follows that a more co-operative horse will result when ridden under saddle.

5 A FOUNDATION FOR FOALS, UNHANDLED AND MISMANAGED HORSES

If the handling of a foal is left until he has developed into a yearling, bad habits may have crept in and then, before making progress, it will be necessary to correct some previously implanted fears and anxieties.

6 THE FIVE ESSENTIAL LESSONS

Handling the body and legs, following, tying up, lungeing and loading are the five essential lessons necessary in any horse's education if its relationship to owner or handler is to be of constant benefit.

4. Equipment and how to use it

During the early part of the 1970s, I was invited to attend a four-day clinic held at a stud just outside a sleepy little town situated in the hills one hour's drive north of Adelaide in South Australia.

The clinic was held by a visiting American trainer, a man of some considerable skill, whose reputation justly preceded him. The clinic was concerned with problem solving in horses. I became fascinated by what seemed to be deceptively simple equipment which, nevertheless, seemed able to make major changes for the better in horses with very bad, and often violent, problems.

A SMALL PIECE OF ROPE

The trainer used a simple length of rope. Horses brought before him changed, quite miraculously, from being unfriendly, confused and disobedient, to willing and co-operative animals. These transformations seemed to happen very quickly. This length of rope, I was later to learn, was called a war bridle and my introduction to it permanently changed my understanding of the nature of the horse and the limits to which he can be trained. The war bridle is central to the advice and handling procedures outlined in Parts Two and Three of this book.

When the war bridle is applied with sensitive hands, it becomes an excellent training aid, producing a light and responsive horse and, in the

A horse reads a direct stare at his eye as a threat, therefore remember to look past his eye, not at it.

Fig. 11 Splicing the eye of the war bridle

vast majority of cases, regardless of the initial problem. It is important to understand that, through the effective use of the war bridle, total control over a horse can be achieved in groundwork. It therefore follows that a more co-operative horse results when ridden under saddle.

FITTING THE WAR BRIDLE

Obtain a 5 m (approximately 16 ft) length of sisal rope 2 cm (3/4 in) in diameter and a pair of sturdy leather gloves. Splice an eye in one end of the rope (Fig. 11). Next, slip the eye end of the rope over his head and down on the offside. Now adjust the rope so that the eye of the rope is hanging down his cheek, about level with his nose, approximately 3 cm (1 in) below the projecting cheekbone. Join the ends of the rope by passing the long end through the eye and drawing it up so that a loop is now formed under his neck, then bring the resulting long end over his nose and underneath the rope on the near side (Fig. 12). The area on the

top of the head is very sensitive, therefore you must take care to place the rope well behind the poll. Gloves must be worn as, at some point, you will need to exert pressure on the rope.

USING THE WAR BRIDLE

Regardless of the problem you are confronted with, whether re-education or the handling of a foal, the animal in question must first learn the *face-up* lesson. (Handling a foal is talked about at length in a later chapter.) By 'face-up' we mean that the horse has, at all times, to keep his front end facing you. At no time is he allowed to turn his hindquarters to you, unless you so desire. This lesson is very important because it forms the foundation for all that is to follow and must therefore be learned thoroughly.

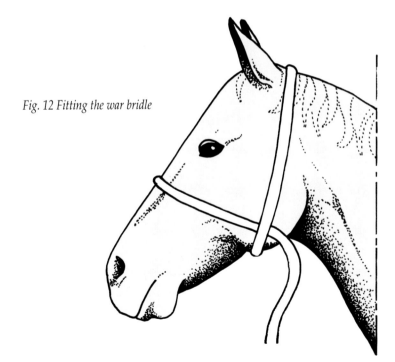

Fig. 12 Fitting the war bridle

Think like a horse - he cannot think like you.

STEP 1

We shall assume that the horse has been caught and that the war bridle is now on. Standing at 90 degrees to his shoulder (this is the best angle to stand at for maximum leverage when tugging) and some 2 m (6½ ft) from him (Fig. 13), take up the slack in the rope and give a sharp *tug*, not a pull, releasing the tension immediately. As a result of this sudden tug, the horse must turn his whole body to face you, not only his head. He must stand freely on a slack rope and face you. If he turns his head only, go back to the first position and repeat the tug. Leaning back on one leg and, at the same time, taking your weight on your hip, take up the slack of the rope first, then tug and release again. If applied correctly, the animal will immediately lift his front feet off the ground and spin to face you as if taken by surprise. Stand still and do not approach him, but talk to him in a calm, even tone, 'Good boy'. (It is *vitally important* that you do not talk *when* you are tugging, as he must not associate the pressure of the rope with you in any way whatsoever.)

What is happening? While turned away from you, the horse felt an uncomfortable pressure on his head. In his mind, you had nothing to do with this unpleasant pressure but, when he turned to face you, he was met with a kind voice and an absence of pressure. In his mind, you have become the alternative to unpleasant pressure. This is the essence of facing

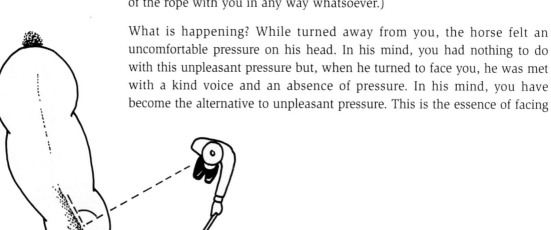

Fig 13. The correct position of 90 degrees to the shoulder

up. The horse has been conditioned to feel safe only when facing you.

STEP 2

Now he is taught to come towards you. Taking up the slack of the rope and remembering not to talk, apply some pressure but *do not pull* (Fig. 14). This pressure is only a feeling of maintaining a constant tension, without any hint of pulling, and requires a sensitive hand. The horse will feel this pressure and you will observe his weight shift to his hindquarters as he resists by leaning on the rope. Despite this, you must maintain the same contact through your hands and give a little tug, slackening the rope immediately you sense that his weight is displaced. You must achieve this release of pressure *before* he actually takes a step towards you. Two seconds later is too late and you will have missed it.

You may need to repeat this several times until the horse has come forward, step by step, until he is right in front of you. Then, and only then, reward him with 'Good boy'. You will observe that his mouth appears a little tight as if he is saying, 'I'm not a hundred per cent sure what it is that you want me to do'. Build his confidence by stroking his face and eyes and watch for the almost immediate response of a big sigh. In addition, he will lick his lips, demonstrating that he has accepted your request. You have now created a *comfort zone* with him. Remember, he

'The leap is either a sudden spring into the air, in which the feet quit the ground simultaneously, or else it is an act compounded of an imperfect rear and kick in quick or slow succession, according to the manner in which it is performed.'
PERCIVALL, 1830

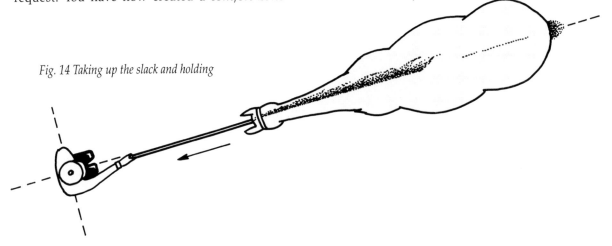

Fig. 14 Taking up the slack and holding

has no idea that you caused the uncomfortable feeling through the rope and he has now placed his trust in you by finding you totally unthreatening. He has worked out for himself that resisting, by leaning on the rope, brought an even more unpleasant feeling and that, by stepping forward, he found comfort. In his mind, you had no part to play in his discomfort. This fact cannot be emphasised too strongly. Had you created anxiety in him by the use of your voice while maintaining pressure on the rope, he would have associated *you* with the discomfort.

STEP 3

This is to verify that the horse will follow you.

Step to the left or right of him, keeping the rope slack, and having at least 1 m (3 ft) between you (Fig. 15). He must begin to follow *with the rope remaining slack*. He must follow you, *not* be led by you. If he does not follow, repeat the previous procedure once again. In a matter of minutes he should be following you around willingly.

STEP 4

The horse must stop when you stop.

Having previously directed the horse through the stage of facing up, this next lesson is quite often unnecessary, as he may already show an initial

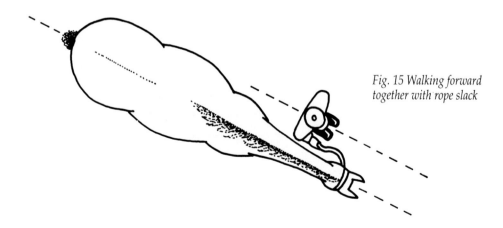

Fig. 15 Walking forward together with rope slack

inclination to stop when you do. However, this cannot always be relied upon. Should he show an inclination to walk on when you have stopped, allow him to do so, making no attempt to stop him with the rope. However, as soon as his head is past your shoulder, take up the *slack* on the rope and give a firm but gentle tug on it. He will be startled, his head will go up and he may turn to the side. Say 'Whoa' in a calm, even tone. If he still keeps walking, give another tug but with more severity and, as soon as he *begins* to slow and stop, slacken the rope and stroke his neck. Now praise: 'Good boy'.

Walk forward again, allowing him to follow on a slack rope, repeat the word 'Whoa' and immediately stroke his neck when he *inclines* to stop. It is important to allow him a second or so to respond to your voice. Do not rush. *You* know what you want but he has no idea. You are effectively guiding him through new ways of behaving.

STEP 5

Among the more uncomfortable experiences that a horse will endure, backing up is certainly near the top of the list.

In this lesson, we show how to achieve willing response from the horse when he is asked to back up. Now that he is following on a slack rope, stand parallel to his shoulder facing his hindquarters. If standing on his left, hold the rope in your right hand and, with your free left hand, reach down to touch him between his forelegs, taking a piece of skin between your fingers and twisting it gently. Do not attempt to push him back while doing this, you are simply giving him an aid by twisting and thereby causing discomfort (much like asking him to walk on, when ridden, by using your heel). By twisting the skin, you have made him uncomfortable. Maintain the twisting until he displaces his weight on to his hindquarters in preparation to back. If he should move forward or to the side in an attempt to rid himself of the irritation, keep the same feel at all times. This is to become the aid to back up and it is important that your hand remains in place until the horse has offered to take a step back. As soon as he *displaces* his weight on to his hindquarters, and not a second later, stop twisting the skin. Repeat this two or three times, keeping him on a straight track. He will soon become conditioned to back up when he sees your hand go down towards his legs, at which point twisting is no longer required.

Now it is necessary to teach him to back up one step at a time but do not hurry him in this. Remember, by keeping his head straight to the front, he becomes totally reliant on you for safe transit backwards. He cannot see behind him. Do not allow him to run backwards away from your hand. You are requesting that he back up one step at a time and only when you give him the aid that commands this.

Depending on temperament, some horses may show a tendency to run back rather than stepping back. Faced with this situation, take a step back and away from the horse yourself and, taking up the *slack* of the rope, give a sharp tug then release it instantly. Apply constant pressure on the rope once again and ask the horse to step forwards to you, (see Step 2). Then, once again, request that he take a step back and you will observe a willingness on his part to carry out the procedure slowly.

TOTAL CONTROL

Observing the horse in a natural situation will reveal that, unless there is absolutely no other way out, rather than back up he will probably spin round to face the opposite direction. Teaching him to back up on command, which he finds uncomfortable, provides another way to demonstrate to him that we have total control over his movements and serves to reinforce our dominant role in the partnership. It is a good idea, therefore, to back him up regularly.

Communicating with your horse is not so much the art of teaching him what *you want him* to do but, rather, what you want *him to want* to do. Achieving this will instil in a horse an increased willingness to learn.

5. A foundation for foals, unhandled and mismanaged horses

DECEPTIVELY STRONG LITTLE HORSES

The question is often asked, 'What is the best age to begin handling?' and, quite often, the person asking the question is shocked by the answer: 'Immediately a foal is able to stand up'. It is widely, but erroneously, assumed that all but essential handling of the foal is dangerous because he is too fragile, small and delicate but this is not so. Foals are, in truth, deceptively strong little horses that have not yet learnt they are stronger than their handler. Herein can be found sound reasons for beginning his elementary training long before the foal feels inclined to test his strength against you. The time you will need to spend with a foal at this early stage should be kept to a minimum, as their attention span is limited to a maximum of 15 minutes.

NATURALLY CURIOUS

This initial training can be most rewarding for at such an early age a foal is naturally curious and, given the opportunity to participate, will learn quickly, developing trust and confidence in the handler. In contrast, one should be aware that if the handling of a foal is left until he has developed into a yearling, the task can assume a more sober aspect. Bad habits may have crept in unnoticed and then, before making progress, there will already be some implanted fears and anxieties to be corrected. For example, simply playing at the wrong time can give an unhandled foal a bad experience. Let us suppose that a mare with a foal is brought in for a trim by the farrier. The mare is tied up but the unhandled foal is not and, becoming bored, begins to play around the yard. Inadvertently, he barges into the farrier and is yelled at for being a nuisance. This is the foal's first experience of aggressive human behaviour. When you are attempting to catch this same foal at a later date, he will remember the shouting and be unapproachable.

INITIAL HANDLING

A brief word of caution on handling is appropriate here. Before you walk boldly into the loose box, paddock or yard with the idea of catching the foal, consider life from the foal's perspective for a moment. At this early stage in his life he knows only the security of the mare, so there is obvious value in endeavouring to simulate her movements and touch as much as possible during your own initial handling of the foal. Aim to reduce any unpleasantness to a minimum so that he will not dislike the experience of being touched.

STEP 1: APPROACHING

First, tie the mare up in a corner of the box or yard. The foal will follow her naturally. It is not important which side of the mare the foal is on as you are only going to touch and stroke during the first encounter. With the mare secured, gradually approach the foal, talking constantly, and keeping your voice at the same level, never raising it. Make your approach towards his centre in a confident manner (the foal is unlikely to kick). There is a midway point at which you may stand where he will remain stationary. If you go too near to the front, he will step backwards; too near to the back and he will run forwards. It is therefore essential to locate this spot, at which he appears unprovoked and remains stationary.

Maintain your position at this point for up to ten seconds, then step back or retreat *before* the foal takes any steps away from you. Approach confidently again, focusing on the area that leaves the foal unprovoked and stationary. It is important not to look directly in his face, in particular his eye, but rather to 'read' the signals that he will convey to you as nervousness, such as any tenseness in his muscles, head up and turned to the side, a shifting of his weight and the movement of his legs. If any of these signs are obvious to you, move back again *before* he moves away. If, on the other hand, his back and hindquarters appear relaxed and he remains stationary, or has an ear turned towards you, you will be able to approach closer to him than before. Remember always to retreat *before* he moves.

Talk all the time, keeping your voice level, even and quiet. The approach must be carried out confidently and without rushing. If, during this initial approach and retreat technique, the foal moves forwards or backwards, allow him to do so, making absolutely no attempt to stop him with outstretched arms or by voice command as he understands neither of these signals.

STEP 2: HANDLING

Having gradually reached the point where the foal is now accepting you and you are able to stand for 30 seconds with no indication from him of insecurity, the next stage is to place your hand on his rump. At this point, it is important to make your touching reassuring by simulating the action of the mare as she would place her neck and head across his body in order to convince him there is no danger.

Once more, make your approach quietly and confidently, remembering to talk constantly. Stand as close as possible to his side and slowly stretch out your arm, touching him with a firm, yet gentle, feel. Scratch him rather than stroke, much like a mare nuzzles a foal to give him reassurance. At this point he may shoot forwards, startled by the touch, and

'Gruel is made from oatmeal, either with hot or cold water, in the latter case hardly deserving the name, but being the form in which it is too often given by ignorant and careless stablemen. To make it properly, one pound of good oatmeal should be carefully stirred up with sufficient cold water to form a thin mixture of the consistency of cream, which will take nearly a quart. This is then stirred with three quarts of boiling water, and the whole kept stirred over the fire till it thickens, when it is to be set to one side to cool, being given when about lukewarm. It is an excellent restorative for an exhausted hunter, and careful grooms provide it ready-made against the master's return from hunting.'
THE HORSE IN THE STABLE AND FIELD, J.H. WALSH (1883)

must be allowed clear access to the mare's side for security. Always allow him clear passage back to this *comfort zone.*

Try again. He should be steadier this time and may even begin to enjoy the scratching. When he indicates with his body and face that he is relaxed, stop scratching, take your hand away and retreat once again. Now make the approach again, remembering to talk in a quiet, level tone, this time scratching for a longer period of time. Maintaining a firm, yet gentle, touch, begin to ease the palm of your hand over his rump to his back. Be alert for any anxiety signs, remembering always to retreat while he is in a relaxed mode and before he responds in a negative manner. In easing your hand further along his back to the wither, lay your arm across it and, at the same time, put a little weight behind it. In this action you are simulating the mare in the act of putting her neck over the foal. When he has totally accepted this handling, finish the lesson and walk away.

STEP 3: APPLYING THE ROPE

On the second day, repeat the previous procedures, reinforcing the earlier lessons if necessary. You will be quite surprised to find that he remembers the experiences of the day before as rather pleasant and will respond readily. Have a rope with you this time and, repeating the same procedure of touching, move closer to his wither and neck. Remember, it is still of primary importance to retreat regularly as, by doing this, you are demonstrating that no threat whatsoever is offered by your presence. Soon, and at the same, very relaxed pace, you will be able to graduate to stroking his ears and face, but if he shows any fear at any time, you must always return to the previous stage in handling.

Remember that what he learns now, he learns for life, and this fact makes it imperative that he should learn well and without fear the first time. When you are able to lay your arm successfully across his neck, take the eye end of the rope in your hand and lay it across also. In his mind, the rope will seem to be an extension of your arm, therefore make no fuss about doing this. Go slow. Keep the foal relaxed by talking and scratching.

STEP 4: FACING UP

The next stage is to have the foal come away from the mare and face you. Threading the long end through the eye of the rope, which is now visible below the neck on his other side, draw it up so that the resulting loop around his neck is kept loose but manageable. So as not to frighten the foal with unnecessary movements of the rope, it is recommended that the reader should follow the illustrations for the fitting and adjustment of the rope in 'Equipment and how to use it'. The war bridle must be correctly placed prior to giving the foal a face-up lesson. He is now to leave his only security, that of the mare. During this sensitive stage, it is vital that you appear as no threat to him whatsoever, for you are about to become his alternative security. Remember to talk to him only when he faces you, using a calm, quiet tone. Having secured the rope as illustrated, position yourself facing the foal, approximately 2 m (6½ ft) from him and at a right angle to his shoulder.

At this point, you must ask a handler to take the mare away to another corner of the box or yard. Seeing the mare move away, the foal will naturally want to follow. Maintaining your own original position and leaning back slightly to keep your weight through your hip, take up the slack in the rope and, applying a little pressure, allowing the rope to 'stretch' as he steps forward. Feeling this pressure may cause him to squeal a little but if you give a gentle, but firm, tug, he will easily be turned to face you because of his small size. His response will still be to turn back immediately to the mare, so you must repeat this tugging again. *On no account* talk when actually tugging on the rope. This initial stage is won by patience. The foal will feel insecure and it is most important that you indicate to him through your voice and body position that you represent no threat.

STEP 5: COMING FORWARD

As soon as he is 'faced up' to you, approach him in the same confident manner as you did when he was with the mare. Walk two steps towards him, talking all the time, and then retreat. If he pulls away, tug gently at

If circumstances force you to stand at the rear of a horse, in order to avoid being severely kicked, stand very close to the hind leg.

the rope, remembering *not* to talk at that time. Once he has accepted this situation, prepare him to come forward by standing in front of him approximately 2-3 m (6-10 ft) away. Now take up the slack in the rope, maintaining a 'holding' feel. If he resists this tension through the rope by leaning back, apply slightly more pressure and tug, but do not *pull*. (Pulling is a continuous tension, tugging is not.) When you tug with the rope, he will jump, his front legs lifting off the ground, but he still may not come forward. If this is the case, tug again, as he must not be 'rewarded' by a release of the pressure until he has come forward. Having applied a stronger tug, he is likely to come forward a step or two. Reward this instantly with your voice and by releasing the pressure on the rope. Step forward with calm movements and touch his face. If he pulls back, apply light pressure once more and tug on the rope again.

After a few minutes of using this procedure, he will come to accept your hand on his face and move forward (to you) quite readily. It is important to understand that he does not know that it is you causing his discomfort through pressure on the rope. Maintaining vocal silence during the application of pressure on the rope ensures that you are not associated with the foal's experience of discomfort.

Foals are naturally inquisitive and you may take advantage of this to allow him to verify your friendliness. When he appears comfortable, bob down on bended knees and allow him time to smell your hair and face, which will assure him that there is no danger from this unfamiliar human presence. It is no coincidence that when allowed this privilege he will accept you all the more readily. Once he is comfortable about allowing you to handle him thoroughly, remove the rope, allowing him to return to the mare. The lesson is over.

One way of demonstrating the disassociation you have with the foal and his experiences of the rope, is to observe his reaction when the rope is removed at the end of the lesson. Once he has been released, he will often remain with you, as he now views you as non-threatening. As you move away, he will very often follow. The mare will call to him and, having turned his head to her and found no pressure as before, he will trot back to her side and the waiting milk bar. He will be exhausted by all these new experiences and, having fed, may sleep.

STEP 6: FOLLOWING

The next stage entails the first lesson in following and must be viewed as an extension of the previous lessons. Re-confirm these by repeating the steps that the foal has already learnt, always returning to any stage that might require reinforcing if he shows resistance or insecurity. Now, placing yourself in front of, and facing, the foal, ask him to come forward by applying a little pressure on the rope, rewarding with your voice when he does so and then allowing the rope to slacken. Now it is your turn to step back, 'stretching' the rope if necessary. By these actions you are asking him to follow. Go slowly, one step at a time, rewarding with your voice immediately he begins to follow you.

This lesson is relatively simple. Before long he will be following you anywhere, irrespective of where the mare is tied up. On occasions, he may attempt to return to the mare and it is vital to be alert for signs that suggest this might occur, giving a sharp tug (with *no* talking), at the point when he turns away from you, then rewarding instantly with your voice and stroking his neck as he returns to the original following position. As he becomes more attentive and is following you willingly, begin to adopt a different body position, so that you are facing in the direction in which you are walking, unlike before when you were stepping backwards. Achieve this gradually while you are walking as any sudden change in your body language would be confusing to him. Remember, he does not know that he is now to walk beside you so it is important to reward him constantly with your voice and to stroke his neck, encouraging him into this new following position.

Teaching the foal in this way will achieve rapid results and a co-operative, relaxed animal. Should he fall behind at any time, apply a sharp tug then slacken the rope, repositioning him near your shoulder and rewarding him once again. Never work him for longer than 15 minutes as the mental demands of these lessons are quite exhausting for youngsters.

It is recorded that, in 1883 'a strapper (or helper), be required to use his hands never his head, and wages paid be from 10s to 14s per week'.

45

The most important lesson that he has now learnt, at this early age and without pain, is that he cannot escape by pulling away. Additionally, you have created several *comfort zones* for him and, as his training continues, he will regularly return to these for security.

STEP 7: YEARLINGS AND ONWARDS

The foregoing are simple lessons to prevent the dangerous habit of a horse turning his hindquarters to you when approached in the yard at a later date.

Of course, you may not have the opportunity to work with a foal. Yearlings and mature horses who have had little or no handling require considerably more work than a foal, as unwanted habits may have been imprinted on their minds through mismanagement. These habits need to be eliminated quickly from the horse's mental file of conditioned responses. Generally, such horses will not have had the face-up lesson and, if approached in their box or yard, can turn their hindquarters towards you as though confronted by an unwelcome intruder.

STEP 8: FACING UP IN THE YARD OR SCHOOL

Whether handling a foal or a mature horse or re-educating an animal with a 'problem', it is essential that dominance and respect are accepted by the horse. This can only be achieved by teaching him to face up in the yard or school. This method uses a home made 'flag'. To make the 'flag', take 50 cm (20 in) length of dowling rod and secure a plastic bag to it (it is important to use a noisy bag).

Having placed the horse in a yard or school, allow him time to trot around to familiarise himself with the numerous smells and to satisfy himself that there is no escape route. Now enter the yard with the flag motionless at your side, placing yourself in the centre and allowing the horse to trot round you. If he shows *any* tendency at all to turn his hindquarters towards you, lift the flag and shake it, creating a noise. Do not do this with the intention of frightening the horse by chasing him. Simply stand still and do not talk. Having shaken it twice, stop using it for a moment, giving him the opportunity to turn to face you. If he continues to trot around, shake it twice again. Use the flag only when he moves away from you. Having made a noise with it, lower it to your side. Should he stop and turn to look at you, *reward* him with a quiet, level voice. Reward him in this way whenever he turns his eye to look at you, even although, at times, his body may be parallel to the fence and at right angles to you.

You must realise that the horse has no idea that you are causing the disturbing noise. All he hears is an unpleasant sound when moving away from you. The principle behind the use of the flag is similar to that of the war bridle. It is very important *not to talk* when using the flag as doing so would immediately link you with the noise. Continue in this way until the point is reached where the horse is stationary and facing you.

Now begin to approach him in a quiet but confident manner, walking towards his wither rather than his head. Avoid looking directly at his eye, as this would prompt him to move backwards. In approaching, do not stretch out your arm to touch him. Keep the flag down at your side. Be alert for signals that indicate that he is likely to employ the fear and flight response, such as shifting his weight on to his hindquarters in preparation to turn or go forwards, folding back his ears and turning or lifting his head. He should be relaxed, standing square on all four feet and looking at you with a relatively quiet eye. Walk two steps towards him, talking all the time, and then, after 30 seconds or so, retreat backwards again, always being prepared to use the flag if necessary. Stay alert. Having reached the point of being able to walk within touching distance of him, stop the lesson for a few hours, leaving him to think about it.

When you return to the yard or school again, he may initially display dominance by turning away but you will find that by using the flag once or twice, it will be possible to walk towards him and that he will prove quite passive. When within touching distance, allow him to sniff you, remembering to keep talking at all times in a calm, even voice but always be ready with your flag should he become startled and trot off. Now bring your free hand up to touch his neck for a few seconds, using an open

Always hold a horse's leg by the toe and not the foot. In this way the horse senses no restraint.

hand and a firm touch. Stroke firmly, but *do not* pat. Now retreat by stepping back, then making the approach once again, repeating the previous touching procedures. Do this a number of times until he has accepted you willingly into his space. Before long, you will be able to stroke him on the neck and crest, using a firm but gentle touch. *Do not* pat him. (I have never seen a horse pat another horse and have grave doubts as to whether they enjoy it.) Having satisfied yourself that the horse is relaxed and has accepted the handling, finish for the day. Make a hay net available and leave him alone.

The following day, repeat the previous procedures, using the approach and retreat technique, and now touching his neck, crest and face. Only when he has accepted your hand on these areas should you prepare to equip him with the war bridle. Place it on his head in the same manner as described for the handling of the foal. Now position yourself at a right angle to his shoulder, about 2 m (6½ ft) away. Take up the slack on the rope and tug, then slacken the rope immediately. If you are positioned correctly, his front legs will be lifted off the ground and he will be turned to face you. Talk to him immediately he is facing you, with the rope slackened. Step towards him, watching for fear and flight responses. If he does go forwards, take up the slack in the rope and give a firm tug, but do not pull. It generally takes two or three tugs to get him to face you. *At no time should you raise your voice or talk to him* when tugging the rope. Talk only when he faces you. By doing this, you are creating a secure area or comfort zone which he enters when in this face-up position. You are establishing dominance by exhibiting that you are stronger than he is. Although he may weigh in excess of half a tonne, he has no idea of his strength and this must apply throughout his education. The war bridle will achieve this and with great efficacy.

From this point on, it is a matter of continuing to handle him. He now has the beginnings of respect for you. It is important to remember that he will respect no other animal, including humans, unless they are seen to be above him in his perceived pecking order of herd hierarchy. He is conditioned by evolution to respect the herd leader and, in the same way, he must respect you too.

6. The five essential lessons

The smallest documented horse was a Falabella mare measuring 38cm (15 in) and weighing approximately 11 kg (24 lb).

1 HANDLING THE BODY AND LEGS

The single most important reason for being able to handle a horse's body and legs is psychological in nature. It allows us to achieve total dominance in our relationship with the horse, at all times and for reasons of control and safety. We condition the horse to respond with acceptable behaviour.

Having introduced your horse to the war bridle and a willing acceptance of your hand, now move on to the handling of his entire body, including his legs, working both sides equally. The majority of people, being right handed, prefer to begin working on the left side of the horse, so we will begin there. Coil the rope in your left hand, using the right hand to stroke with. It is important to keep enough rope between the horse and yourself to enable you to tug should he attempt to move away from your hand (about 1 m (3 ft) is sufficient). First, stroke his neck, head and ears. If, at any time, he does pull away, give a tug on the rope, releasing the pressure immediately and saying 'Whoa' when he begins to stand still and stroke (do not pat) his neck to reassure him. Return to your handling, correcting in this way only when he moves away and is not accepting your hand. This correction technique must be immediate, so be sure that you have the appropriate length of rope available at all times.

Touch him across the back, maintaining a contact with the flat of your hand, remembering to let out some of the rope to enable you to progress towards his hindquarters. It is important that he stands still as you handle him. You must always be alert for signals that he might move or pull away so that you can correct by tugging with the rope immediately. Talk to him continually in an even tone of voice. It is fundamental to your success in this handling procedure that your mental attitude is one of assuming that you have total control. By adopting this frame of mind, you will remain calm. You must exercise patience as this will have a significant effect on the horse's responses.

Return regularly to his head to reassure him that it is perfectly acceptable for him to stand still and not follow you. By the language of your body position, he will learn when he is to stand still and when to face up. Now run your hand over his hindquarters and swing his tail gently. By doing this you are asking him to release all tension in this region. When his tail does become relaxed, so will he.

It is important that you move regularly to his other side in order to prevent him from becoming a 'one sided' horse. Horses have a 'split' brain. What they see on one side is not computed as being the same on the other side, therefore each side must be worked equally. When stroking his quarters, go all the way down to his hocks, also running your hand down the inside of them. He must accept your hand anywhere on his body.

PICKING UP THE FRONT FEET

He can now be taught the signal for picking up his feet, which will eliminate you having to pick them up for him. You have already rubbed your hand down over his legs, inside and out. The next step, of lifting the feet, must carry on from here. Stand at his shoulder, facing his rear, with the rope in your right hand if you are on his left side. Run your hand down his foreleg and, at the same time, lean gently into his shoulder with your shoulder. When your hand reaches the tendon at the back of the cannon bone, squeeze or pinch it until he picks up the foot. Immediately he picks it up, reward him with 'Good boy', but do not attempt to hold the foot. Repeat this exercise until only a light touch is necessary before he responds by lifting up his foot.

Now catch the foot by the toe and hold it for four or five seconds, bending it up a little and then, having given it a wiggle to warn the horse that you are about to put it down, allow the weight of the leg to take it to the ground. (Do not drop the foot as it will bump on the ground, giving the horse a fright.) Repeat this procedure on the opposite side, remembering to reverse hands. After these initial lessons, begin to hold the toe for longer periods, lifting it forward and then folding the leg up to the elbow before releasing. Remember, if he pulls away, correct him immediately by tugging on the rope but *do not* shout at him.

PICKING UP THE HIND FEET

The same procedure applies for the hind legs, except that you will obviously need a longer length of rope between your hand and the horse's head. Hold the rope in your left hand and, at the same time, maintain a 'feel' on the rope but without tension. Lean your arm on his rump (have the feeling that you are about to push him away) and position yourself as close to his body as you can. Adopting this stance gives you the advantage that, should he attempt to kick, there is less risk of you getting hurt and you will also be able to push him away quickly with your left hand. Having laid your arm across his rump, run your right hand down to his hock and on to the cannon (Fig. 16). Pinch or squeeze the tendon on the back of the leg while leaning in with your left hand to place him off balance (this will make him feel more inclined to lift his leg). As he begins to shift his weight on to the opposite hind leg, place your hand over the cannon and bring the leg forward.

Repeat this exercise several times until he is familiar with the process and then, at the point of raising his leg, move your hand down to hold it by the toe (do not grab at the leg as he will pull away). Hold for a few seconds, progressively increasing the time, so that you can move the foot into different positions as a farrier would when shoeing. Again, if he shows a tendency to kick or pull away, correct severely with the rope, *not* your voice. Now repeat this on the other side, reconfirming contact with

The oldest documented horse was a Cleveland Bay cross which lived to 62 years. The greatest recorded age for a pony is 54 years.

Fig. 16 Position of handler when lifting hind leg.

him regularly by stroking his body and face. When he has accepted these experiences totally, quit for the day.

CURING THE HABIT OF LEANING

A problem that often occurs is that the horse may choose to lean on you after he has picked up his hind leg. There are two ways to cure this habit. If, having taken his foot in your hand, he begins to lean, release the foot quickly causing him to become unbalanced. The second cure is recommended if he continues to lean. Tie one front leg up with a leg strap or stirrup leather and let him stand on three legs for around ten minutes. He will then learn to balance himself on three legs. To apply the strap, bend the leg up to his elbow and secure the strap so that he cannot drop the leg. If a leather is not available, a length of thick rope will suffice but wire is not acceptable. When applying this remedy, place the horse in a safe yard or box with soft ground (this will prevent him getting hurt if he should fall) and leave him to adjust to balancing on three legs.

Do not be concerned if the horse falls over as horses can rise quite successfully on three legs only. Quite soon he will learn by his own actions to stand on three legs. Remove the rope, asking him once again to lift his leg. You can expect to see a marked difference in his acceptance of this procedure but, if not, repeat the lesson for a slightly longer period of time. He will eventually come to accept his own weight and keep his balance on three legs.

2 FOLLOWING

WHAT WE MEAN BY FOLLOWING

In effective training, it is essential that the horse should learn to follow wherever the handler chooses to go. By this, it is meant that the horse follows you willingly as you move in any direction, without tension on the lead rope or reins.

We must not try to *lead* him anywhere; he is to follow. Horse and handler are still connected by a rope (either a lead rope or a war bridle), the difference being that there is no pressure or weight on the rope between them. This eliminates the 'push-pull' characteristics of resistance, so typical of faulty handling.

Having already educated him to come forward to a slight pressure, teaching him to follow is relatively simple, provided that three basic rules are constantly observed during the lesson:

- Make it understood to him, through reward, exactly what his position is to be.
- No matter where you go, he must follow and without any hesitation.
- Keep him focused and attentive at all times.

MIND OVER MATTER

The horse does not know where his body position is supposed to be in relation to yours, therefore you must show him. Remarkably, seeing these relative positions clearly in your mind will tend to transfer the same information to him, because what you wish to happen will be indicated through your own body language. The mind is a powerful tool and it is true that the horse has an uncanny ability to know what is going on in yours, so be very careful what you think about and the emotions you entertain while handling him. If this concept is new to you, consider it for a moment. Have you ever had to catch a particular horse in a herd that is in a large paddock. Almost immediately you focus on that horse, he trots off. Now try deliberately turning your attention away from that particular horse. He will settle again, allowing you to walk towards the group and, sensing no further threat from you, he will rejoin the group where he is easily caught.

THE LESSON BEGINS

Having fitted the war bridle on the horse, proceed through the previous lessons in 'coming forward'. Now, while keeping a light feel on the rope, position yourself in front of him, releasing the pressure immediately he steps forward. Having achieved this, take one step backwards, keeping the rope slack and applying pressure only if he displays any reluctance to

'If the resistances of young horses spring from a physical cause, then this cause only becomes a moral one by the awkwardness, ignorance, and brutality of the rider.'
METHODS OF HORSEMANSHIP, SIR F.B. HEAD (1863)

begin following. He should come forward to you quite readily. If he does not, you have (a) hurried through the previous lesson, (b) his attention was not totally focused on you, or (c) you did not give adequate reward as he stepped forward. Always look to yourself first for the causes of an error, not to the horse. After all, you are the teacher, while he knows nothing and waits to be taught. If he does not respond by following, take up the slack once again and give a sharp tug to gain his attention.

In stepping back, gradually begin to reposition your body so that you are facing the point where you intend going. He will be slightly behind your shoulder now and you need to introduce him slowly to this new position. Now imagine standing still with the horse beside you (there should be 50 cm or 20 in of rope between you). This distance allows enough space to discourage the bad habit of 'crowding'. Your shoulder should be level with the middle of his neck and both of you should be facing forward. Imagine this and let the horse know, through your mind, that this is where he is to be. Step forward with a slack rope, giving him a little tug if he refuses to follow. As he jumps forward, reward instantly with an even voice and stroke (but do not pat) his neck. You are showing him what to do. Keep walking forward and tugging (but not pulling) on the rope, if necessary, to maintain the following position. It will require just a few minutes' work in this fashion for him to realise where he has to be.

As soon as he is walking beside you and has a degree of confidence in his step, ask him to stop with your voice. Do not attempt to stop him with the rope. Visualise both yourself and the horse stopping together in unison. Stop walking yourself and, as you do so, say, 'Whoa', maintaining a quiet, even tone of voice. He is likely to take a step ahead of you and you should allow him to do so but, as he gets beyond the 'zone' or position you have created, give a tug on the rope to correct him and he will then return to the comfort zone parallel to your shoulder. Reward him with your voice and stroke his neck. Walk forward and stop again, remembering to maintain a *slack* rope. It is important not to stop him with the rope, either by taking up the slack or by pulling, as it is essential that he learns to stop simply because you have. He is to follow *you*.

This lesson is fundamental to sound horse handling and all the training that follows. Repeat the lesson several times, having patience and maintaining an even, quiet mood throughout. The strategy for turning in a new direction is the same as it is for stopping. If the horse is positioned on your right and you begin turning by stepping to the right, he will, at first, be likely to swing his head towards you, not having been shown the signals to respond to by turning his body to the right. This can be avoided by raising your right hand towards his left eye, blocking his vision to the left, which has the effect of turning his head to the right (Fig. 17). At the same time, move your right hand towards his left eye in a flicking motion and he will turn to the right (it is vital that you do not bring your hand into contact with his eye). This action has the effect of turning his eye away from you and focusing his attention to the right, inducing him to turn. Immediately he begins the turn, lower your hand, raising it only to indicate to him the direction you intend. As he becomes familiar with the signal, it will only be necessary for you to lift your hand in the direction of the turn. This will then be a sufficient signal for him to comply. Always maintain your own correct position. Keep yourself and your horse focused on the lesson, requesting that he follow you. As you progress, take him through various obstacles, such as through water and over ditches and plastic. When you have completed this work correctly, he will follow you anywhere and at any speed. Remember that practice *does* make perfect.

3 TYING UP

THE REWARD OF BREAKING FREE

The hills are alive to the sound of 'My horse won't tie up!' In truth, however, all horses are capable of being tied up, provided that they are given sufficient and *correct* education. This complaint actually means that the horse will tie but will not remain tied. He has learnt that to pull back when tied up, breaking whatever restraint is holding him, is to become free from the resistance he feels. He 'reads' this breaking free as instant reward, by discovering that to pull back brings immediate relief. When

'Clover is greedily devoured by all horses, and fattens them quickly, but it is not suited to those cases where a cooling diet is wanted to relieve inflamed joints.'
THE HORSE IN THE STABLE AND FIELD, J.H. WALSH (1883)

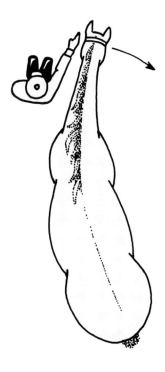

Fig. 17 Blocking the horses vision with hand to effect a turn to his right.

teaching to tie up, therefore, it is absolutely essential that the equipment used is unbreakable, because once he has learnt that to put pressure on the rope is to get away from that pressure, he will undoubtedly repeat it.

This lesson can be taught to the young foal, with the added advantage that he will have had no previous opportunity to find out that his strength can release him from the restraint. Having gone through earlier handling procedures, the foal has learnt to come forward to light pressure, therefore tying up will come quite easily to him and with little or no fight. This same procedure is also used for an older or previously mismanaged horse but, of course, he may resist for considerably longer and with greater strength. When the appropriate precautions of using unbreakable and correctly adjusted equipment are followed, the lesson is quickly learnt.

TWO CARDINAL RULES

A variety of methods is used in teaching a horse to tie up correctly. We shall describe two of the more common ones here. No matter which one is selected, it is important to establish two basic requirements:

- Carefully select an area that is perfectly safe, free of wire, rocks or any other items on the ground that could cause damage to the horse. A railed yard or small paddock is ideal.
- The horse should be tied to a very stout, upright, well-anchored post

Fig. 18 Tying the bowline knot

with no protrusions. Should your facilities be limited to a paddock, select a tree which has a fork in the trunk at about the height of the horse's wither. Again, be sure to clear all debris well away from the tree. This includes any branches and twigs protruding from the tree that might damage the horse. (Simply stated, you must make the area very safe. If the horse should hurt himself during this lesson, it will set up complex handling problems for later on.)

METHOD 1

It is important to take steps to prevent the horse from damaging himself should he plunge forward when tied. Wrapping feed bags or similar around the tethering tree or post is an effective way to achieve this. If your upright post is set away from fences, dropping several tyres over it, ensuring that he bumps into these and not the post, is also effective, but do make sure that they are tied together. You can then actually tie the horse to one of these tyres.

The equipment that you will need is a headcollar with buckles and dees and 5 m (16 ft) of thick nylon rope which has been rubbed down with coarse sandpaper to remove the slipperiness. We recommend learning to tie a bowline knot, as it will be necessary to use one during this procedure (Fig. 18). The bowline knot is the only one that can be used for this method as it is easily loosened no matter how hard the horse pulls back.

Begin applying the rope to the horse's head by sliding one end up through the dee on the side of the headcollar (it is not important which side), then over the top of the head and down through the dee on the other side, ensuring that the rope sits well back from the poll. You should now have a long end and a short end. Tie these two ends in a bowline knot that sits snugly at the back of the chin, taking care not to allow the knot to slip down under the mouth (Fig. 19). The long end is now passed through the back of the noseband of the halter. It must then be wrapped twice around your selected anchor – the fork of the tree, tyre or post. Make sure that the lower wrap comes from the horse and the upper wrap is fed to the handler, which ensures that the rope will not tighten around the post.

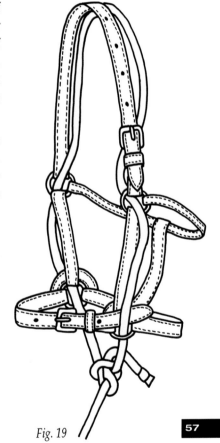

Fig. 19

Wrapping the rope around twice (and not tying a quick-release knot) allows the force from the pull of the horse to be on the wraparound and not on the release knot, which would, of course, tighten. Having wrapped it around twice, pull it snug and, keeping a tension on the long end, secure a quick-release knot (Fig. 20). Allow about 1.5 m (5 ft) of rope between the horse and the post and tie it at wither height.

It is fundamental to the success of this lesson that the horse is now left alone. Do not generate nervousness in him by encouraging him to pull back by waving sacks etc. He may well stand for a few moments before starting to turn, go back or attempting to face you. Do not go to him. *Allow him to pull back.* The rope will not break and neither will the tree or post. He has to come forward to obtain relief from the pressure he feels. Do not be tempted to go to his aid unless he gets into a situation where he has his leg over the rope and you can see no way for him to release himself but do this *only* if absolutely necessary. Generally, if left unaided, the horse will sort it out. Some horses that I have worked with have lain or sat down, or just plain pulled back, for what seemed an eternity. The do come forward eventually but the lesson is that they learn

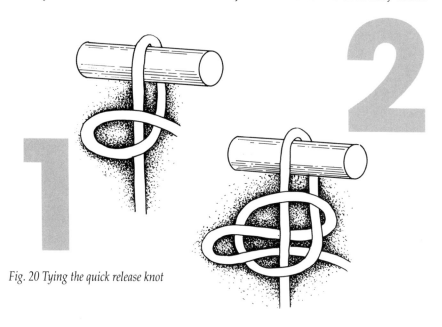

Fig. 20 Tying the quick release knot

by their own actions. Generally, they pull back two or three times and then, giving up, stand quietly. Never flap at him or hassle him at this time as this will only create a nervous horse as he will feel trapped and may not cope emotionally.

METHOD 2

This is virtually the same as before but, instead of using a rope, a hessian sack is folded lengthways several times so that it becomes approximately 8-10 cm (3-4 in) wide. A hole is made at each side, through the combined thicknesses, 10 cm (4 in) from the end. Now take the same nylon rope used in the first method and thread it through the bag, tying it using two half hitches, through one end (Fig. 21). Loop the sack over the neck of the horse and bring it under his jaw, run the other end through the holes you have made and secure it with a further couple of half hitches. Take the long end of the rope through the back of the halter and secure it to a sturdy fence rail, post or tree (Fig. 22). For horses over 18 months of age, where considerable strength has developed, this method has the advantage of distributing more evenly the pressure that results from pulling back.

Other methods are explained in Part Three, the section on problem solving.

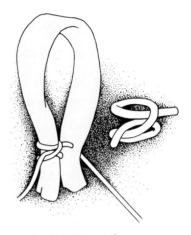

Fig. 21 Setting up the hessian sack for use in the tying up lesson

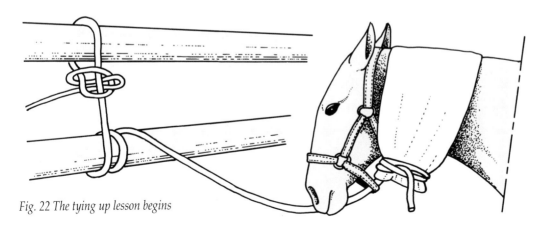

Fig. 22 The tying up lesson begins

*W*hen tying up your horse in a
float or trailer, it is useful to
remember that the quick release
knot is better placed near the side
door for ease of access.

4 LUNGEING

QUALITY CIRCLES

It is an odd thing to teach a horse to go round and round in an endless succession of circles and it is easy to see that this exercise can be either immensely boring for the horse or enlivening for him and worthwhile for you. We lunge horses not only because it teaches the horse to go forward without the security of the handler's presence, but also because it teaches him to obey voice commands, so important for those first rides under saddle. It has the additional advantage of enabling you to continue working the horse when he is suffering from saddie sores etc. and is an excellent way of teaching the unbroken horse to go forward. Further, it is of benefit when beginning light work after the horse has been out at grass or off work for some reason and also enables the horse to be worked if the rider is temporarily unable to ride.

WHAT WE ARE ASKING

Not all horse owners are blessed with a round yard or pen to work in and it is not really necessary to have this facility for the initial lungeing lessons. In fact, when using a round yard or pen, the handler tends to rely on the curve of the area to keep the horse moving in a circle, whereas in a paddock or school you must actually teach him to listen to your commands, which is an excellent way of teaching you to teach properly.

Initially, fit the horse with the war bridle and take him into the area that you have selected to work in. So far, he only knows how to follow, to come forward to a slight feel on the rope, to face up and to tie up. All that we ask of him now is to go forward independently. As with previous lessons, knowing clearly in your own mind what you want is of great benefit to the horse. Picture clearly 'I want to lunge the horse' and your body language will reflect that thought. Think for a moment what this request means. It is that the horse should work on a continuous 360-degree circle while you stand still at its centre.

GETTING STARTED

First, you will need to demonstrate that there is no risk for him in going forward ahead of you, as, until now, the horse has only been taught to follow. Go to the position that you normally adopt for him to begin following. Stop him and then position yourself behind his shoulder and inclined towards his quarters (Fig. 23). You are showing him, through body language, where you want him to go. He will feel insecure at first so reward him with your voice at the slightest move towards what you are requesting. Be content with one or two steps at first. Plenty of patience is required for this lesson if it is to be taught correctly and in a way that allows the horse to finish refreshed and happy, rather than hot and confused.

Picture him moving away from you. At times he will turn his head to come towards you but you must keep asking him to move forward by raising your right hand and, if necessary, your left hand, focusing it towards his left eye which, in turn, will prevent him from looking at you. When, eventually, his eye is diverted to the right, he will go forward. As soon as he takes a step forward, reward him instantly with the sound of your voice. Keep the tone steady: 'Good boy'. Maintain the same body position and ask him to keep moving forward. It does not matter at this point whether he stays on a circle or not as long as he is moving forward. Tell him to 'Walk on' and, as

Wearing gloves greatly increases control, while also avoiding the painful experience caused by rope burns.

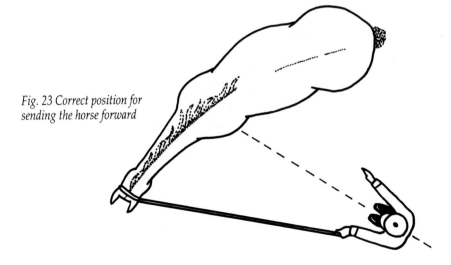

Fig. 23 Correct position for sending the horse forward

he walks forward, reward often with the same, even voice.

If, at any time, he begins to turn in, encourage him forward with your right hand and raise your left hand, which will prevent the left eye from looking at you. Now step in front of him (this being his cue to stop) and say, 'Whoa' (Fig. 24). Make the phrases 'walk on' and 'whoa' distinct from each other, so that he distinguishes them clearly. If he does not stop, ask again, then, when he shows an inclination to slow down, reward him with your voice. As soon as he stops, go to him and stroke his neck. It is important that he is *not* allowed to turn into the circle, an annoying habit that can quickly creep in when allowed to.

Step away and back towards his quarters, then ask him to walk on again. Allow about 2-3 m (6-10 ft) of rope to come between you, and no more, or you may lose control. If he begins to trot, immediately make this your decision by saying 'Terrot', making your voice rise to a slightly higher tone. Allow him to trot a couple of strides, then ask him to 'Walk on' again. If he fails to come back to a walk, give a tug on the rope then, as he slows down, release the rope to encourage him to walk. Repeat the words clearly as he enters the new gait. When he is going forward and stopping happily, begin to bring him on to the line of a circle (Fig. 25).

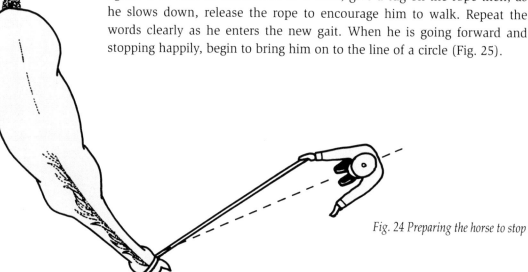

Fig. 24 Preparing the horse to stop

Stay in walk with no more than 2 m (6½ ft) of rope between you. Give regular little tugs on the rope to keep his head turned slightly inwards, but keep him moving forwards. The circle will not be perfect at first, so be content with a little progress. Repeat these routines regularly, remembering to work both sides equally. Stop him often, do some stroking of his body and pick his feet up. Finish on a good note, well before he is looking for ways to avoid the tasks. Horses sour quickly if kept going round in endless circles.

At this point in the proceedings, do not encourage him to canter as he is not sufficiently balanced to execute a small circle at this early stage. If he should canter, allow him to go forward for two or three strides then give a tug on the rope to bring him back to trot. As he progresses, lungeing can become quite varied as the size of the circles can be changed and executed in different areas. You can ask for a forward-moving trot and then bring him back on to a smaller circle, thus teaching him to balance and to use his quarters and back. Taking him forward out of the circle at times will allow him to lengthen the trot.

Ten minutes of lungeing each way is equal to one hour of normal riding.

'*M*anners *make the man, but still more the hunter, and without good manners no horse can be considered fit for a gentleman to ride to hounds.*'
THE HORSE IN THE STABLE AND FIELD, J.H. WALSH (1883)

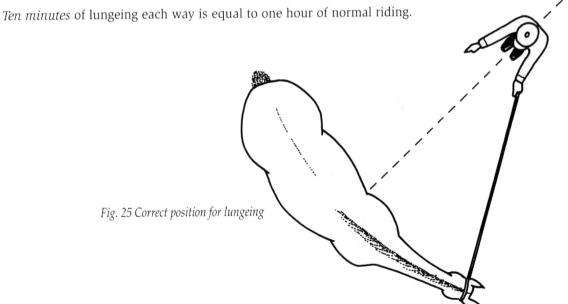

Fig. 25 Correct position for lungeing

When loading a single horse on a double float or trailer, load to the side nearer the centre of the road for greater stability when towing.

5 LOADING

GETTING THE PREPARATION RIGHT

Before beginning to teach effective loading, it is a useful exercise to think about what we are really asking the horse to do. Specifically, we ask him to walk up and forward into an enclosed area.

It is important to ensure that the lorry, trailer or float is as non-threatening to the horse as you can possibly make it. Inside, it must be free of all projections. Also check the floor underneath the rubber matting, to see that the wood is intact and not rotted or fractured. Horses have been known to break through a broken floorboard, travelling in panic for some distance before the driver has realised what has happened. As a point of maintenance, check the floorboards frequently. Also make sure that the inside walls on either side have a padded section that stands proud of the wall by around 10 cm (4 in) and to about waist level. This will ensure that the horse's sides are never in direct contact with the true wall of the vehicle. This also provides some degree of support for the horse when the float or trailer goes round corners. For the same reason, the chest rail should also be padded and the central divider should be of the kind that is easily removed. The ideal central divider should extend to the floor, either as a solid timber half-wall or, better still, should be made of rubber, allowing the horse some movement of his legs. As a note of caution, this central divider must never end just above floor level as it will trap a horse's foot.

LITTLE THINGS MAKE ALL THE DIFFERENCE

A double float or trailer should sit on a double, long axle for superior road handling as this will give the horse and driver a much smoother ride. The single float or trailer does not give as smooth a ride to the horse although, surprisingly, there is not a great deal of difference in the weight of single and double floats or trailers.

When the horse walks up the ramp, he has no idea that the ground will level out again as he moves further in so, ideally, the entrance should be light and spacious, encouraging him to step forward. Check that the groom's door is open as this, in his eyes, is an escape route. He will be more secure about going in if he believes he can see a way out. When using an enclosed vehicle, check that the roof is high and made of a semi-transparent material, allowing a maximum amount of light to illuminate the inside. When using a float or trailer with a roof, make sure that this covers the entire roof area, not just a quarter roof at the end where the horse's head will be. In truth, in countries where the climate permits, most horses are more comfortable when travelling in a completely open float or trailer (one with no roof at all). Many horses with deep-seated fears that have resulted from accidents will generally travel quite happily in an open float or stock crate. This is because they have good all-round vision and this mode of travel helps them to maintain their balance, enabling them to find their 'sea legs'.

If your horse completes a task correctly, do not keep on repeating it.

CLIMBING THE ROOF

By way of caution, it is worth mentioning, if only briefly, an unfortunate accident that occurred to a horse travelling in a float with a quarter roof. It is not clear what startled him initially nor how he came to be in the position that resulted but, according to the owner who was driving the towing vehicle at the time, when the float was finally brought to a stop the horse was found with his front legs over the quarter roof, which, in turn, had collapsed and pierced the window at the front of the float. The horse suffered horrendous injuries but, strangely and as is usual in accidents of such severity, he remained very calm throughout the ordeal and allowed his many helpers to disentangle him. Remarkably, this same horse, once healed, walked straight into another open float, never once giving the slightest indication of any bad memories of travelling in previous times.

In guessing the sequence of these events, it was assumed that the horse had pulled back while in transit and, finding himself entangled in the rope, had reared, coming down over the rooftop. Some people believe that certain types of part-roofed floats are not safe.

SETTING THE SCENE

The positioning of the float or trailer is important. It must be placed so that the sun is shining on the back of the vehicle, illuminating it inside. Should the sun be behind or to the side of the float, the horse will be walking from direct sunlight into darkness and his eye will struggle in making adjustments in order to cope with the deep shadow of the float's interior. Be careful to select an area that is free of fences, bins, trees and obstacles in general. A paddock or large yard is ideal. His first loading lesson needs to be a pleasant experience and this largely depends on you checking everything very thoroughly. Having parked the float or trailer, which must remain connected to the towing vehicle, lower the tailgate and remove the central divider. Also remove any projections at the back and inside, such as bolts and any pieces that are liable to swing. In other words, remove anything you think could cause injury to the horse or to you, or that could get in your way.

THINGS NOT TO DO

The loading lesson is usually forgotten in the early handling of the horse or else it is assumed that the horse will somehow 'be OK on the day', and will just walk in or maybe even follow another horse in. All of these assumptions are incorrect. Nor is there much merit in leaving the float in the paddock, assuming that the horse will gradually become accustomed to its sight and smell. The disadvantages of this far outweigh any advantage. Because it will not be hitched up securely, there will always be the risk of it tipping forwards or backwards.

Other 'back porch' wisdom has found some owners leaving a bucket of feed inside the float with the idea of encouraging the uneducated horse to walk inside in order to feed. They do, of course, but it seems that many horses, although feeding inside a trailer in the paddock, do not necessarily associate this experience with actual loading.

There will always be the ever-present possibility of an unsupervised animal injuring itself, regardless of how careful you may have been in the preparation and safety of the float or trailer. Horses have an uncanny way of searching out something on which to injure themselves and it always happens when you have just 'popped out' for ten minutes.

THE POWER OF POSITIVE PSYCHOLOGY

We shall assume that the horse being loaded is doing so for the first time but the method used here can also be of use with a horse requiring re-education. This method assumes that the horse will *wish* to load, rather than being *forced* into the vehicle. To achieve this (which is largely a psychological stance on the handler's part), the most important thing is for the handler to adopt a positive and confident attitude. Being possessed of ample patience and, perhaps more importantly, remaining totally impartial throughout the lesson, will achieve great progress. There is no place here for aggression or impatience. The horse will immediately detect these feelings. If you approach this with the thought, 'Gee, I hope I can get him in' the fact is you probably will not. It is very common for people to have this feeling of doubt when preparing for a horse show. They become increasingly tense, nervous and apprehensive and the horse that usually loads with ease now refuses to move. In a case like this, if you take a deep breath and push the doubts to the back of your mind, he will probably walk straight in. Remember always that it is *your* moods, both positive and negative, and not his, that have the dominant influence in all these situations.

BACKING UP – YOUR HORSE'S REVERSE GEAR

Before beginning, check your horse's reverse gear – back him up. Many years ago, I went to pick a horse up and was in a bit of a hurry – my first mistake. My second was that I didn't check the horse's reverse gear. This horse loaded well but, on arrival, refused to back out, not because he was stubborn but because he had never been taught to back. Teaching to back up before loading will avoid great embarrassment on arrival! A trust must already be formed between the two of you before this lesson is begun; that is, the horse must feel totally secure in the knowledge that you will, on no account, put him in an insecure situation. If previous lessons and handling have been carried out correctly and thoroughly, he will trust you totally.

'*The attainment of "good hands", by which is to be understood a light and delicate handling of the reins, is, or ought to be, the aim of every rider. The most delicate mouth in the world is soon spoilt by bearing heavily on it, as is too often done by grooms, and, indeed, by the average run of our horsemen.*'
THE HORSE IN THE STABLE AND FIELD, J.H. WALSH (1883)

67

Teaching to back requires that the war bridle be fitted. Face the horse's rear but a little to one side of his head and have the rope coiled in your right hand. Now reach out your left hand and gently twist the skin between his front legs – but *do not* push him back. Immediately he adjusts his weight, in preparation to move back, take your hand away but only if he inclines backwards in this way. If he should move forwards, keep twisting the skin. You are simply giving a cue by creating discomfort. It is for him to work out that reversing away from the twisting sensation brings relief. Quite soon, you will notice that it only requires you to lower a hand in the direction of his chest before he begins backing. Do not pinch or twist severely; aim to keep it light. As he backs, confirm and enforce the correctness of the action with the words 'Back up', remembering to keep the same calm tone in your voice. Keep him straight. Should he swing his quarters to the right, incline his head to the right also (and vice versa, inclining his head left to correct a left swing), asking again that he go back. This will have the effect of swinging his quarters a little to right or left, thereby enabling you to maintain his straightness. Ask for small steps, slow and straight. Show him you have control by a positiveness in your actions.

THE LESSON BEGINS

He must now be asked to step towards you. This is achieved by taking up the slack on the rope and maintaining a constant feel but not a pull. The horse will then step towards you. Release pressure on the rope (which, of course, will happen automatically if you are simply holding and not pulling the rope) and reward by stroking his face, eyes and mouth. Again, and gradually getting closer to the tailgate, ask him to step towards you while continually reconfirming the trust and security between you.

A point worth noting is that when loading a foal or weanling, and at the point where you take the first step on to the tailgate, you should bob down slightly on bended knees, maintaining the same level as before in relation to the foal. Otherwise, when standing on the tailgate you will be higher than before and, in the foal's mind, become a quite different personality to the one he recognises. If you adopt this position you will make the foal much more comfortable about taking that initial step upwards.

SOUND PROOFING

Having got as close to the tailgate as possible, all that you are going to ask of him is that he stand straight and accept the noise you create. By stepping on to the ramp and keeping the rope *slack*, you will be able to move your foot up and down so that the ramp produces a noise. The horse may react in alarm to this, jumping back, snorting or perhaps both. If he attempts to move away, take up the slack in the rope, keeping hold until he steps forward once again. In moving away, his face and mouth will tighten because of the insecurity he is experiencing but when he comes to accept what you ask of him, the muscles of these areas will relax again, he will give a sigh and begin chewing. When, through these signals, he shows you that he has accepted your request and is secure once again, you can proceed to the next step. It is very important that he faces the noise you produce on the tailgate. As soon as he does come forward again, be there to give comfort to him by stroking his face.

THE COMFORT ZONE

Watch carefully for signals that indicate he is relaxed and accepting what is happening. You are creating a comfort zone for him. It is fundamental to the success of this training that you make him feel secure by coming to you. Should he require any 'correction' at a later time, through tugs on the rope, he will quickly remember and step back to the comfort zone that you have established as his security. If you are to achieve notable success, the creation of this bond of trust between the animal and your-self is imperative.

Remember, the horse does not know that he has to step up on to the tailgate. In his mind, this is an obstacle that he cannot get over. Through your persistence in holding the rope, correcting with sharp tugs as he goes to the side or moves backwards, instantly releasing when he comes

In 1831, Mr Osbaldeston rode 320 km (200 miles) over the Newmarket racecourse using 28 horses, including one hour 20 minutes for stoppages, in eight hours 42 minutes.

Out of 130 winners in the English racing diaries during the 1750s, only 18 were 15 h.h. and upwards.

forward, he will eventually realise that he has to step forward to feel comfortable. He will probably do this quite by accident, perhaps when jumping around while puzzling over what is being asked of him, but the end result is just as valid. As soon as he steps on to the ramp, release the rope and reward him by stroking him. By doing this, you show him that he is safe and secure in the comfort zone and that stepping forward was correct.

BACKING OUT STRAIGHT

This first stage on the tailgate is the most difficult but, once accomplished, the rest of the lesson will come easily. The horse will now be quite happy to proceed the rest of the way up the ramp but do not allow him to do so. He must dwell on the experience of the ramp for a moment or two, before you back him right off. Back him away from the ramp and away from the vehicle, keeping him straight for at least 4 m (13 ft). The reasons for this are twofold. Firstly, it keeps him straight and demonstrates to him that your are in control. Secondly, it prevents another habit from creeping in, that of the horse going off the side of the ramp before he has all four feet clear of it. Now ask him to step forward again and, as he does so, talk to him, maintaining the same tone and pitch of voice. Stroke him but do not pat. Each time, ask him to go a little further up the ramp before backing him out again. Eventually it will be possible for him to walk straight in without hesitation. When he is happy to stand freely in the float or trailer, allow him to sniff and look around but ensure that he stays facing forwards. When loading, he will be following you but when unloading, you must turn to face him, placing you in a position to back him.

When backing him out, allow him to step back only far enough to keep the same distance in relation to you, i.e. keep about a metre (3 ft) of slack rope between you. If you should stop moving, so must he. Put another way, having asked him to back out of the float or trailer, do not walk towards him but, rather, stand still and, by cueing him with your hand to go back, allow him to step back to the end of the prescribed length of slack rope between you. If he steps beyond this point, take up the slack using a feather touch on the rope before applying a firmer feel. He will step forward and the reward is given by releasing this tension immediately. You have been standing still but must now take a step towards his shoulder, giving him the back up cue again and allowing him to take another step back. Ensure that he backs out slowly and under your full control. What you teach him now will stay in his mind for life. For this reason, it is important that you teach him to load and unload both slowly and straight.

CONCERNING TAILGATES

Raising the tailgate is unlikely to present problems as the horse now knows that the float or trailer presents no threat. As a precaution, however, ask an assistant to raise the ramp while you watch the horse's face carefully for any sign of anxiety. Occasionally, shadow changes, created by lifting the ramp, generate minor nervousness, but in the vast majority of cases a youngster will display ready acceptance.

When preparing to travel under normal circumstances, raise the ramp *before* you tie up the horse and, having arrived at your destination, untie the horse first then lower the ramp.

Having taught the horse to load, it is now necessary to pull the float or trailer a short distance with the horse on board. Stay with him in the float or trailer and ask an assistant to drive slowly forward and to turn both left and right. It is unnecessary to take a long journey, a short driveway trip is quite sufficient. Having completed this, unload and finish for the day. Practice the loading/unloading procedure at least once a day but only two or three times in each session. It is this frequency and consistency that will turn the horse into a perfect loader.

'HANDS OFF' LOADING

Always walk in with a youngster as it gives them a keen sense of security. With older horses, however, you should begin asking them to go in independently as soon as they are loading smoothly. (Until now the horse should have been loading with the aid of the war bridle. You should make

Never be fooled by spit and polish; for beauty is only skin deep.

the decision to quit its use only when the horse loads perfectly, going in without a moment's hesitation.) In addition to the war bridle, use a lead rope and, having positioned him at the foot of the ramp, lay the lead rope across his neck, as this will become his cue to go forwards. Now encourage him on by a gentle prodding with your hand at the back of his chin, just where the noseband of the halter sits. He will eventually take a faltering step forwards and you must reward him instantly in an even voice, asking him to go forward again. He will now go in. Maintain your 'going forward' position (i.e. facing the way he is going), keeping your open hand on his back and rump as he steps forward. If he shows any sign of insecurity, step into the back of the float or trailer and stay at the top of the ramp. Stroke him around his hindquarters and gently swing his tail. Keep him relaxed. Again, if he shows any sign of insecurity, go to his head, keeping your hand constantly on him, and then stroke his crest. Back him out and repeat the exercise. Practise it two or three times in one session each day.

'HANDS OFF' BACKING OUT

There will be occasions when it is necessary to load and unload without the help of others and having taught the horse to go forward into the trailer on his own, it is also possible to teach him to back out without needing to be at his head. To do this, it will be necessary to keep the war bridle on and ask him to load on his own. As he moves up into the float or trailer, play out the rope, allowing him to load completely, leaving you with the rope's end in your hand, standing in the rear of the vehicle while still maintaining your 'forward position'. Keep the rope slack.

To back him off the cue you are going to use is, first, an even command 'Back up'. Secondly, take hold of his tail near the end of the dock and tug the hair gently. Thirdly, give a slight tug on the rope. These aids must be given within seconds of each other, so that, eventually, he will back out when you tug his tail. As soon as (and not a second later) he shifts his weight to his hindquarters, quit these aids and allow him to step back. If he stops and goes forward, repeat the aids.

This lesson, just like all preceding lessons in this chapter, is taught by patience. Your horse starts from a position of knowing nothing; you are his only teacher and master. Remember that he seeks to please.

The essence of all good horse training is that it is a course in repetitions, by which a lesson is implanted. There is no place for force in this principle.

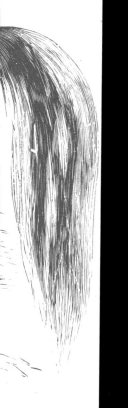

PART THREE

A Guide to Curing Problems

In this third and final section we look closely at common vices, problems and bad habits encountered in horses. Collectively, these problems can be said to occur as a result of earlier mismanagement or stresses related to inappropriate handling, which drive the horse to seek avoidance of a task and are displayed as unacceptable behaviour.

A CAUTIONARY NOTE

Any type of re-education contains an element of danger and risk of injury to the horse. All the methods outlined here have inherent risks as well as rewards and it is for the reader to select whichever feels the most comfortable. If you do feel worried about trying any of these methods yourself, it is strongly recommended that you employ someone who is thoroughly experienced in horse handling.

7 PUSHING, CROWDING AND RUNNING FORWARD

The action of being inattentive to the handler and rushing forward is common in leading, where the horse has learnt through his strength to 'take the lead'.

8 PULLING BACK WHEN TIED UP

A condition in which the horse pulls back persistently, until the rope or halter tethering him to post or rail is broken.

9 LOADING OR TRAVELLING PROBLEMS

Fears that have arisen through earlier experiences may manifest themselves when the horse is faced with the prospect of loading again. Related problems also occur in transit, such as scrambling.

10 FAILING TO LUNGE

The horse rushes, turns in or refuses to go forward when lunged. This condition is caused by souring the animal through the endless repetition of moving in circles without variation.

11 RESISTING THE BRIDLE

Raising or throwing the head high when the handler is fitting or removing the bridle, usually associated with earlier and rough handling.

12 WEAVING, CRIBBING AND WINDSUCKING

Vices which are common to the confined horse and have developed as a release of the stress caused by prolonged inactivity or boredom.

13 BITING

A natural act of aggression which establishes the superiority of one horse over another in the herd environment but is otherwise considered an unacceptable and dangerous vice.

14 KICKING

Like biting, kicking is an effective and natural response used by the horse to establish rank at herd level. The habit of kicking can also develop through rough or inappropriate handling.

15 HARD TO CATCH

A condition brought about when the horse senses no profit in being confined. This can be remedied by a change of approach in handling.

The next four vices, although primarily riding problems, are listed here because they are closely related to initial mismanagement in groundwork.

16 SHYING

A horse's exaggerated response to random objects in his surrounds, and evolving as a habit when confirmed by the concerned reaction of the rider.

17 REARING AND STRIKING

A habit formed when a horse seeks to escape a stressful experience when in confined surroundings that prohibit backing away. An extremely dangerous habit, on occasions proving fatal to both handler and horse.

18 BUCKING

Horses can buck through exuberance, but this can become a bad habit if done while being ridden. Bucking develops through the discovery that a weight or any form of irritation can be removed by a bucking action.

19 BOLTING

The unpredictable occurrence of fleeing from a perceived fear at breakneck speed and motivated through panic.

7. Pushing, crowding and running forward

PUSHING OR CROWDING

The problem

Perhaps the most common problem encountered when handling horses, and the one most easily cured, is the horse that persists in running forward, crowding or pushing the handler. This horse has received no education defining the acceptable distance that must be maintained between himself and his handler. The condition is potentially dangerous and should be addressed without delay.

The cure

To cure the problem of pushing or crowding, first put on the war bridle and give the horse a lesson in facing up, then stand in the ideal following position, with your shoulder level with the middle of his neck. The horse that crowds is apt to look every which way and will certainly not be focused on the handler. Ask him to move forward and, as he begins to lean your way, give several sharp tugs on the rope, releasing the pressure immediately. His response will be to run back. As soon as he is 1 m (3 ft) or so from you, reward him with a calm, even voice but do not talk to him while you are tugging or correcting. Now go back to the original position and, keeping the distance between you, tell him 'Good boy'.

It is quite acceptable to repeat these steps as many times as is necessary and to be quite severe when tugging or correcting. In just a few minutes he will begin to accept the new and correct position. Remember to reward often but only at the right time. The correction must be given at precisely the moment the horse begins to lean and not a second later. If you miss the moment when he begins to lean, you will find it difficult to be in a position to correct fully.

A similar problem to crowding can occur when turning the horse away from you. He either refuses to turn or stops and goes the other way. To cure this, put the war bridle on the horse and stand opposite his neck. Do not walk forward. If you are standing on the left side (near side), coil the rope in your left hand and lift your right hand towards his left eye (Fig. 26). He will only turn the way his eye is facing, so your objective is to divert his look away from you and to the right. Initially, his left eye will be looking at you, so lift your right hand and flick it at this eye (avoiding actual contact with it) and he will turn his head. *Now* ask him to go forward, flicking your hand over his eye constantly. If he stops and runs back, refusing to turn, give one or two hard tugs with the rope and quickly move to his side, continuing to flick at his eye. Immediately he attempts to move away to the right, reward with your voice. Repeat this process several times until he is comfortable with the new command.

This exercise will not make the horse headshy unless you actually strike him with your hand or yell at the same time as correcting. Remember that you are merely showing him, by diverting his gaze, a new direction to take. Quite soon, you will only need to lift your hand towards his face while he is walking or trotting to induce the turn.

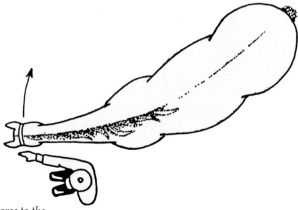

Fig. 26 Diverting the horse to the right by blocking his left vision with the hand.

RUNNING FORWARD
The cure

To cure this problem, it is essential that the horse *be allowed* to run forward into the position that you do not want him in before correcting severely with the war bridle.

With the war bridle fitted, walk the horse forward and, when he begins to run forwards, jiggle or go sideways, tug very hard several times in quick succession, releasing the pressure after each tug. Again, the correction must come at the point when he has just come out of the position that you have set for him.

When he runs forward, the correction is given and he is stopped hard in his tracks, but you must still keep tugging with sharp jerks until he has backed into the correct position. Do not face him to do this but stay in your position and let him find his own way back. Do not be tempted to take him to the position you want – he has to do it himself; that is the only way he will learn. As long as you reward immediately, he will quickly respond.

8. Pulling back when tied up

The problem

This is a common habit among horses which, by pulling back when tied up, have found that they can relieve the pressure of a restraining halter by breaking it. Any horse that has become a habitual breaker of halters is very likely to repeat the vice even after re-education. Therefore, even after giving the lessons described here, all such horses should be tied with equipment stronger than a single lead rope! There are no measures that will offer a 100 per cent guarantee that the re-educated horse can be trusted to tie up without fault every time. There will always be that one time when he tests it yet again.

Cure 1

There are as many as four different cures to the problem of pulling back. The first is detailed in Part Two 'The five essential lessons', and is repeated here in essence, the primary difference being that here we address a problem that is established in the horse. As a mature 'puller' exerts a great amount of pressure on his neck, the first method is an excellent cure.

Regardless of which of the following methods is selected, it is important to establish two basic requirements:

- Select an area that is perfectly safe, free of wire, rocks or any other items on the ground that could harm the horse. A clean, railed yard or a small paddock is ideal.

- The horse is to be tied to a very stout, upright post with no protrusions. If your facilities are limited to a paddock, select a tree with a fork in the trunk at about the height of the horse's wither. Again, clear away all debris from around the tree, including any growing branches and twigs that may cause damage.

Be absolutely sure that the rope used for re-educating a puller is unbreakable. To prevent the horse from injuring himself through plunging forward when tied, wrap feed bags or similar effective padding around the tethering post or tree. If the upright post is set away from fences, dropping several tyres over it will serve to cushion the horse also. If you make sure that the tyres are secured to one another, the horse can actually be tied to one of these tyres. Aim to make it all as safe and secure as possible.

The equipment that you will need for this method is a headcollar with buckles and dees and also 5 m (16 ft) of thick nylon rope that has been rubbed down with coarse sandpaper to remove the slipperiness from it. You will need to be able to tie a bowline knot (Fig. 27). This knot is the only one that can be used as it will not tighten regardless of how hard the horse pulls back. Slide one end of the rope up through the dee on the side of the halter (it is not important which side), then over the top of the head and back down through the dee on the other side.

You now have a long and a short end to the rope. Using these two ends, tie a bowline knot snugly above the chin groove, taking care that the knot cannot slip down under the mouth when the horse pulls back. The remaining long end is now passed through the back of the noseband of the halter. It must then be fed out to the fork of the tree, tyre or post and wrapped around twice, ensuring that the lower wrap comes from the horse and the higher one to your hand. If this is not done, the rope will tighten and prove impossible to untie. By wrapping the rope round twice, the full force of the pull will be on the wraparound. Having wrapped the rope around twice, you can finally secure it with a release knot. Allow about 1.5 m (5 ft) of rope between the horse and the post and, when wrapping the rope around, ensure that it is approximately level with the horse's wither.

Now leave the horse alone. Do not encourage him to pull back by waving sacks at him. Let him find his own way. He will learn. He will probably stand for a few moments before becoming restless, start to turn, go back or attempt to face you. Do not go to him. Allow him to pull back. The

Fig. 27 Tying the bowline knot.

rope will not break and neither will the tree or post. He has to come forward to obtain relief from the pressure he creates by pulling back. In the unlikely event that he gets into a situation where he has, for example, a leg over the rope, and if there is absolutely no way for him to free himself, cut the rope, but otherwise do not be tempted to go to his aid. He will sort it out himself. Some horses that I have worked with have lain or sat down or just plain pulled back for what seemed an eternity. They will come forward eventually but this must be learnt through their own actions. As a rule, most horses pull back two or three times and then give up and stand quietly.

Cure 2

A second method is a virtual repetition of the above and duplicates the fitting of the rope with a bowline as in Cure 1, but with the addition of a harness. One rope sits across the hip and another across the wither, with a third rope around the sides of the horse, all coming together at the chest to form a harness (Fig. 28). This is then joined to a fourth rope using a bowline knot. This fourth rope is taken through the back of the noseband of the headcollar, together with the rope from the first head rope, and both are wrapped around the post or tree. The body rope should be slightly shorter than the head rope so that, in pulling back, he first feels

Fig. 28 Rope harness in position.

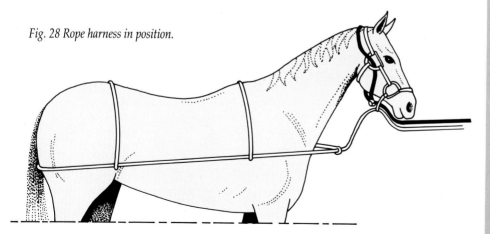

pressure around his hindquarters, followed by pressure on his head from the longer rope. Some horses do not readily accept such harnesses, therefore, when using this method, check first that the horse fully accepts it before using it as an aid to tying up.

Cure 3

The third method uses a rope to form a loop around the horse's body. This is tied with a bowline. The loop is placed behind the last rib, just in front of the hip. Now take the long end of the rope up between the front legs and through the noseband of the headcollar, feeding it out before wrapping it around the post (Fig. 29). It is important that this rope always goes through the headcollar because it will then prevent the horse from turning his head and will keep him facing forward. The body rope may slip forward when he pulls but this will not alter the effect. The pull from this method acts directly on the barrel of the horse and its sensation encourages him to come forward quite readily.

Fig. 29 The pull from this method acts directly on the barrel of the horse.

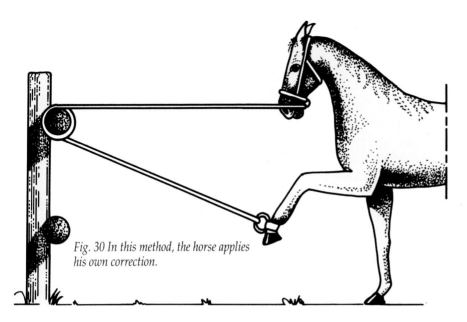

Fig. 30 In this method, the horse applies his own correction.

Cure 4

The fourth method requires 6 m (20 ft) of unbreakable nylon rope. Attach one end of this rope to the halter using a bowline knot secured at the back of the jaw. Position the knot well up into the crook of the chin so that it will not come forward over the horse's mouth as he pulls back. Now pass the rope over a sturdy, unbreakable fence rail before bringing it back down to one of his front feet. Place a hobble strap (on to which a metal ring is securely attached) around the pastern of the horse and then attach the rope to the metal ring. In pulling back, the horse's front foot will be lifted up and forwards (Fig. 30). In this method, the horse applies his own correction.

FEAR OF THE ROPE

A case may be encountered where a horse will pull back because of a genuine fear of the rope and not from the anticipated relief he receives from breaking free. Generally, this type of horse is unlikely to pull back to the point of the rope breaking but only to the point of 'stretching' it. At some time in his past, this horse may have had reason to back away from

a rope after being mishandled and he now displays a fear of the rope, not of being tied up.

The cure for this problem is straightforward and requires the use of a yard or box but not a paddock. Leave a length of rope dangling from the halter (sufficiently long to drag over the ground) and leave him to work out for himself that the rope causes no harm. When he has settled (usually after about ten minutes), attach a longer rope to the headcollar and take the long end of this over a fence rail (do not tie it), keeping hold of it yourself. Now put steady pressure on the rope but *do not* tug. The horse will undoubtedly respond by stretching backwards. As he does so, allow the rope to go with him (rather like playing a fish on a line). Show him that pulling and stretching do not get rid of the thing he is most frightened of. Once he has backed away from the fence rail, allow the end of the rope to fall from your hand. As he continues to back it will trail across the ground in front of him.

His response will be to snort and back up. Do not go towards him as he must not associate you with the rope. Simply leave him alone. Only when he has accepted the rope by relaxing and chewing his mouth should you go to him, returning him to the post to repeat the process. He may 'free' himself several times but each time he will begin to accept the rope more readily and eventually will not attempt to pull back at all.

9. Loading problems

The problem

Owning a horse that has a 'loading problem' causes anxiety for both horse and owner. The more common problems associated with loading are scrambling, rushing back, refusing to load and going to the side. All are habits born of incorrect handling, abuse and even bad driving but all, with the exception of scrambling, are curable, responding well to sound re-education through patient handling.

RUNNING BACK

It is often said, incorrectly, that the horse with this problem actually loads very well when, in fact, he usually rushes into the float or trailer, squashing himself up against the chest rail. It can then be quite difficult to get him to shift his weight from this until, eventually, he runs back out at breakneck speed. Even when the horse is loaded, he is not at all happy about the experience. Everything about him spells tension and discomfort. His mouth is tight, he definitely will not eat and is usually preoccupied in looking around. We can surmise from this that he has been given a beating at some time in his life for refusing to load initially, then hit for good measure once loaded, or, in coming off, he has slipped and maybe fallen to the side.

After eventually loading, the horse may have become so frightened and confused that, when starting to come out, he has again been handled roughly and has slipped. Now, not only does he want to get the coming out part over with as quickly as possible, but the going in is connected for him with the experience of coming out. When dealing with this problem, it is important to avoid thinking 'I must stop him from going back'. There are two reasons for this. Firstly, it is physically impossible to stop half a tonne of muscle from backing. Secondly, you will need to turn your mind and body signals to 'Come forward please'. This is important because

once the going in has been slowed down by way of a lesson, the coming out will also begin to improve as you take his mind off reversing and focus it on going forward. The first course of action, therefore, is to make the horse feel more secure in your presence and to begin trusting you.

Put the war bridle on the horse and work with him some distance from the float or trailer. Ask him to come forward and, if need be, give a sharp, once only, face-up lesson. Use no voice, just positive action and reward, asking him to come forward to you, and stroking his eyes, face and mouth. Keep your hand on him until he relaxes and displays a soft eye, takes a deep sigh and starts a chewing motion. This is a sign that he has accepted you as dominant and someone to trust. Back him up regularly, turning him through the back up, and showing him that you have total control and that he is quite safe in doing these exercises at your request. Stop and reward often by stroking his face and eyes. After ten minutes or so, his face should be dropping quite low and he will have given himself over to you totally.

Having previously removed the divider and all other protruding parts that he may injure himself on, have him follow you to the float or trailer. Stand in front of him and ask him to come forward to you by stretching the rope between you. Step back on to the ramp and put your weight on it so that it moves up and down. Do this until he has totally accepted the resulting noise and movement. Now back him up five paces before taking him back to the ramp. Step on to the ramp and ask him to come forward, stroking his face and mouth when he does so.

It is important that you remember to keep the rope *very slack* unless you are asking him to come forward. You wish him to come to you because he sees you as his security. Bob down a little to remain level with his face and ask him to put a foot forward on to the ramp. Reward him when he does so. Now back him up off the ramp, keeping him straight. Continue in this way: half a step forward, followed by plenty of backing off. It is very important to back him off before he becomes uncomfortable, thus lessening his feeling of being trapped. For this reason, the instant he puts any weight on his hindquarters, back him up immediately before he has the opportunity to decide himself. Make backing up your idea, not his.

When you have advanced to the point where his front feet are on the floor of the float or trailer and his hind feet are on the ramp, allow him to remain there for a few seconds until he feels balanced and comfortable. As soon as he relaxes, back him two paces down the ramp but not completely off. Now come forward again. You are, in a sense, playing him like a fish on a line, each time drawing him a little further in. If he should suddenly run backwards, allow him to do so. Do not attempt to stop him, you cannot, but allow the rope to stretch with him, keeping a slight tension on it at all times. He is only testing to see what will happen and nothing will because you are not going to do anything unpredictable.

Immediately ask him to come forward to you again, stroking his face when he does so. If he repeatedly runs back, on the third time allow him to get all the way out of the float or trailer, then give a very sharp tug on the rope. This action will bring him straight to you. Do not speak or even indulge in any feelings of anger towards him when correcting him as he will detect any such changes in your mood through the rope. (His senses are *very* subtle.) Remain very neutral. Be there for him when he comes to you. As you are his security, you will be able slowly to change the fear-producing tape that he has playing in his head because of the previous abuse, to one that allows him to walk in and out of the float or trailer because he wants to.

Continue in this way, reeling him in and out, backing him up often and always keeping him straight. Be both consistent and persistent in what you ask of him. This re-educating process can take up to two hours and, thereafter, must be practised frequently for short periods at a time. If he shows you that he feels safe and secure in walking in and out the first time, quit and put him away. It is the frequency of loading that will see him performing as he should.

GOING TO THE SIDE

The problem of going to the side when loading begins as a tiny step in that direction. The handler then steps off the ramp to place the horse

back at the front of the ramp and tries again to bring the horse forward. In doing this he inadvertently gives the horse the small reward of a rest and the formation of a habit begins. Before long, that tiny step has extended into a total swing to the side. He is now given a couple of tugs on the lead rope (didn't hurt a bit!) yelled at (insecurity setting in) then another rest while somebody runs to get the lunge rope so he can be hauled in. He leans on the rope and gets away. He has now learnt that he is stronger than the handlers, they give up and he is put back in his box or yard (another reward!). If this sounds familiar, it is a problem that is easily corrected.

A comfort zone must be offered to the horse, showing him that areas outside of this zone are very uncomfortable and, having been shown, he will again assume the correct position for loading, i.e. straight and forward.

Put on the war bridle and bring the horse to the front of the ramp. Stand in front of him and ask him to come forward. In stepping forward, he is likely to swing his hindquarters to the side. Immediately take up the slack on the rope and give rapid sharp tugs but do not pull. Keep tugging, releasing immediately he shows an *inclination* to swing his quarters back to the front of the ramp. Reward with your voice ('Good boy') and, reaching out, touch his face. Stroke him. Ask him again to come forward. Half a step is fine but should he at any time begin going to the side, apply quick sharp tugs, releasing instantly when he begins to come to the front of the ramp again. If he should swing his quarters back to the ramp and then begins to go the other way, the same rule applies – rapid sharp tugs, only releasing when he is lined up at the front of the ramp.

This position is the comfort zone mentioned earlier and he must find this zone for himself. Show him you approve by releasing the pressure when he *inclines* to the 'front' position, rather than waiting until he is actually there. Encourage him instantly. In a very short time – 10-15 minutes – he will quickly come to realise where his comfort zone is and will constantly return to this area.

REFUSING TO COME FORWARD

A fear of loading or travelling in some horses, produced by earlier experiences, can be triggered by the sight of the float or trailer over 20 m (22 yd) away, and finds the horse refusing to come forward. He stops, snorts and pulls back, trying to remove himself as far as possible from the presence of the vehicle.

Place the war bridle on the horse's head. Assume an attitude of ignoring the float or trailer (do not even see it in your mind). Also ignore what the horse does and do not attempt to 'lead' him. Allow the rope to run its length and walk past the float, maintaining a gap of 10 m (33 ft) from it. Ignore his jumping and pulling away and keep walking past the float. As soon as you are past the float or trailer, stop but do not attempt to stop the horse. He will, by this time, be jumping around nervously, showing a definite inclination to rush. Allow him to do this, then, as soon as he is beyond the float or trailer, turn your body towards him, quickly placing yourself in a position that puts you at an angle of no less than 45 degrees to the horse. Step back with one leg, putting your weight into your hip, stretch the rope and tug firmly. The horse will be stopped abruptly in his tracks by the power of the war bridle and will then swing to face you. Tell him 'Good boy'.

You will now be fairly close to the float or trailer and, as he turns, he will be confronted with this 'monster'. Maintain a firm feel on the rope without pulling. His weight will be on his hindquarters, ready to spring backwards, and he will be totally focused on the float or trailer. Tug again to bring his attention on to you. Keep a feel on the rope and he will step forward, releasing the pressure himself. Again tell him 'Good boy'. Continue repeating this procedure until he steps forward freely, seeking the security of the comfort zone that you have created.

Now observe his face, ears and eyes closely. If his ears and eyes begin to turn away from the float and he puts weight into his hindquarters, this is the first indication that he intends pulling away (fear and flight response). Instantly give a correcting tug on the rope so that he remains focused on you and not on the need to run from the float. Repeat this simple procedure

until you have manoeuvred him around to the tailgate of the float or trailer.

In this situation, it can happen that the horse begins to rear in an attempt to avoid going forward. Great care and agility on the handler's part are necessary should this dangerous habit begin. The horse may previously have learnt that rearing benefited him because he was then able to get away from the handler who used only normal loading equipment such as a headcollar and leadrope. Rearing begins with the horse's head going up and the front legs following, so allow the rope to extend as far as necessary without letting go of it. Do not attempt to stop him, as pressure on the rope at this point is likely to send him over backwards so that he will fall hard to the ground with the possibility of severe injury or death.

Instead, the instant his front feet touch the ground again, take up the slack on the rope and, while applying sharp, rapid tugs, step smartly towards him so that he is forced to back up for at least 15 m (49 ft). At no time during this correction must any sign or feeling of aggression be present in the handler (the horse will not associate the correction with you unless you act, feel or talk aggressively). Now stop tugging, allowing him to focus his attention on you. Ask him to come forward by stretching the rope a little and, when he does so, stroke his face and watch for an almost instant response, a big sigh and the licking of lips. Have him follow you back to the float and again ask him to come forward.

Do not hesitate in repeating the procedure if he should rear again. It is important to re-establish the slow backing as soon as possible, to show him that it is correct for him to back but only when you make the decision. From half to one hour should see the horse accepting the float or trailer as non-threatening. He will then follow you inside.

SCRAMBLING

Scrambling is occasionally referred to as 'climbing the wall' and is caused by one of several factors. The horse may have experienced an accident while travelling, may have travelled with a fidgety horse or the driver of the towing vehicle may have taken corners too abruptly. Scrambling can also be developed by anything that might cause the horse to slip or fall in transit. *The condition is incurable*.

Strangely enough, the scrambler generally loads and unloads perfectly, not indicating that there is a problem until put into the same situation that caused the problem originally, when he will climb the wall of the float or trailer, fall over backwards and practically turn himself inside out. Recently, I came across a horse requiring re-education, which loaded perfectly and gave all the indications that he was happy and secure. It was not until the tailgate was simply touched that the problem became obvious. Just hearing the noise of the tailgate lifting caused him to throw himself over on his side. It was suggested to the owner that he acquire a stock crate and, as the horse was important enough to him, he did this and the horse travelled well from then on.

The scrambler needs to feel totally unconstrained so the more room he is allowed, the better he will travel. As mentioned earlier, there is no known cure, but it is possible to make the horse much more comfortable by giving him some freedom in transit. For instance, an open float or trailer is significantly better for this purpose than an enclosed one. Also remove the divider and allow him as much headroom as you can by lengthening the amount of rope when tying up. Better still, use an open stock crate with open sides, where the horse can walk in and travel whichever way he considers to be the most stable. Transporting a scrambler in a lorry or truck, where he is positioned sideways, gives increased security by allowing him to balance himself.

CAUTION

An erroneous and dangerous assumption is that the scrambler will travel better if confined, that is in a single float or trailer or by having a divider that goes down to the floor to 'brace himself' against. In fact, any type of constraint will induce the horse to resist uncontrollably and promote his scrambling into darker problems. While it is possible to make life more comfortable for the scrambler, a total cure is not possible.

FALLING IN IT

Many years ago I worked for an old breaker who took an unusual approach to the re-education of a horse in his care. One of its problems was to run back when unloaded from a float. It was a very severe case. The old breaker trucked him to the jetty, backed up the truck and let down the tailgate. As expected, the horse flew out and promptly found himself in the river. From that day on, he came out very carefully and the problem never occurred again.

This, however, is drastic action and not recommended to the inexperienced. There are times, though, when some problems require a little more than quietly working in the yard and then ingenuity can be used to great effect!

10. Failing to lunge

RUSHING

The problem

Rushing becomes a habit when a horse is put on the lunge to 'get the sting out of him', or can also be caused by him being chased around the lungeing circle with a whip. In both cases, the habit has evolved by focusing the horse's attention on running from a whip. Inducing a young horse to canter round and round in a meaningless journey of circles can eventually lead to permanent damage to the animal's legs. In any event, cantering should not be allowed on the lunge circle until a horse is working correctly in walk, trot and halt and going through these transitions quietly and with confidence.

The cure

In all corrective work on the lunge, have the horse dressed in a war bridle. A lunge whip is not a necessary tool in re-educating but can certainly be used later, when refining the art of lungeing, by encouraging the horse to engage his hocks and use his back.

When working on the problem of rushing, it is essential to go back to educating as if it were the first lungeing lesson, simply asking the horse to move forward at the walk and halting frequently. It is important that he stays out on the circle and that it is the handler who goes to the horse, not the horse to the handler.

If, the trainer having said 'Whoa', the horse refuses to go at a slower pace, repeat the command and give a gentle tug on the rope. If there is still no response, drop your hip to put weight in it, take up the slack in the rope again and give a very sharp tug, literally stopping the horse in his tracks – always do this as he is about to break into canter. This sharp tugging will have the effect of sitting him back on his hocks. Immediately ask him to go forward again at the trot. Should the pace begin to quicken,

repeat the remedy by dropping your hip and giving a further tug. Do this as often as is necessary. The time taken is very little but the results pay handsomely, with the horse settling down quickly into a pace that you have selected. As he settles into a comfortable trot, ask for walk by giving gentle tugs on the rope and rewarding immediately with your voice, then tell him to 'Walk on'. Step in front of him for the halt, go to him, stroke his face. In a few short sessions, the horse will lunge correctly.

TURNING IN
The problem
The problem of 'turning in' becomes apparent quite early in the lungeing process. Having been rewarded with a halt, the horse turns in to face the handler for the reward of a rest. It becomes an irritating habit in which the horse continually turns in and stops in the middle of lungeing on the circle. It must be vigorously combated and not allowed to occur at any time while lungeing.

The initial lesson is given using a length of rope of approximately 3-4 m (10-13 ft) between the horse and the handler, enabling more control over the pace and size of the circle, and establishing the correct line for the horse when asked to stop. As this lungeing lesson continues and the arc is gradually increased, it will soon become automatic for him to stay on the line of the circle without turning in. You must go to him when you command him to halt. Initially, having got the horse to move forward, keep the circle small enough so that you are able to touch him by taking two or three steps in his direction. As soon as he turns his eye to you (but not his ear), take a step towards him and flick your hand at the inward-facing eye until he hops forward again. Reward with an even voice.

If he has a bad habit of turning in quickly and trotting towards you, watch for the signals that he is about to do this as indicated by his body movements. When he is about to turn and come inwards, he will first look at you, then shift his weight to his hindquarters and drop his shoulder into the circle. At the very first signal, give a very sharp tug on the rope and get behind him, encouraging him on with your voice by 'Good boy' but only do this when he shows the slightest indication of moving forward. If he persists (and some do by trotting fast to the centre), you must give several sharp tugs until he shows a reluctance to turn inward again. As soon as he begins to slow down, encourage him forward again, trotting him on for a few more steps before halting him. If you give him frequent stops and rests in this way, he will move forward more happily for you.

Remember to keep these sessions to a maximum of 20 minutes and to work on both reins in that time.

11. Resisting the bridle

HEAD TOO HIGH

The problem

Virtually all problems presented by the horse when bridling can be traced to earlier errors of management and, of these, rough handling is the most common. However, the horse may also have suffered a knock to the teeth with a metal bit or have received rough grooming of the head.

The cure

The first objective must be to convince the horse that putting his head down need not be fraught with danger, but can also be an extremely pleasant experience. Put on the war bridle only and handle the horse carefully around his head, searching for and locating the area that causes him to raise his head high. (This is the area of his head that will be focused on later in the handling.)

Stand in front of him and begin by stroking his face, eyes and mouth in a similar way to that in which you would handle a youngster, i.e. firmly yet gently, frequently removing your hand before the horse withdraws his head from your touch. If he pulls away or puts his head up, apply slight pressure to the war bridle rope but not a pulling down pressure (it should have only a 'holding' feel). The *instant* he drops his head in response to this, even by as little as a couple of centimetres, release the 'holding' pressure. Continue to stroke and also begin placing your fingers in and around his mouth and gums, again putting pressure on the rope if he attempts to pull away. It is very important that the rope pressure is released the instant he drops his head. Quite soon, he will lower his head when you ask.

When he is responding in this way to a light feel, apply firm pressure just behind the poll with the tips of your fingers and, when you can get his head as low as you require, begin introducing the bridle. Do not talk to the horse but allow your hands to do the rewarding.

To put on the bridle, first remove the bit as this will be tackled later as a separate exercise. Standing beside him on the near side, place your right hand over his head, asking him to lower it by using the pressure of your fingers near the poll. If he does not respond to finger pressure, use the rope, but apply it as lightly as you possibly can, remembering not to pull downwards. Holding the bridle in your left hand, place it carefully on his head, lifting the headpiece well above the ears and remembering to fold these forward gently. It is important to keep your hand on him at all times, using the rope to correct if he does pull away. When reversing this process (removing the bridle), lift the headpiece forward over his ears, being careful not to bump his eyes. Only when he has come to accept these movements totally, is it time to introduce the bit.

Because it is possible that he has felt the bit bump his teeth in some past encounter, you should first use the rope in place of a bit until he is

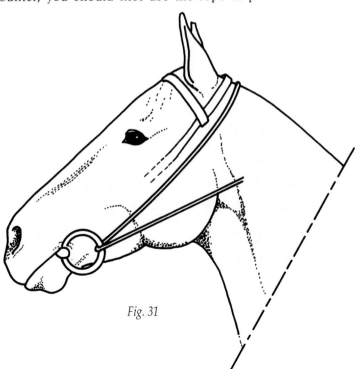

Fig. 31

opening his mouth freely for the rope. This process shows him that there is no pain when he is asked to open his mouth and encourages him to accept the bit more readily. To open his mouth, cup your hand, palm uppermost, under his lower lip and place your thumb inside his mouth on the bars of the mouth at the back of his front teeth where the bit will sit (you cannot be bitten as there are no teeth there).

Using your thumb, apply a little pressure and, as he opens his mouth, slip the rope in, allowing him to chew on it. Hold the rope up in his mouth, beyond the front teeth, maintaining a slight upward pressure and then, allowing the rope's weight to drop, let him expel the rope by movements of his tongue. If he should raise his head, do not then allow the weight of the rope to drop but maintain the upward pressure. Only when he is comfortable about this process (and not before) should you use the bit. Do not attach this to the bridle, however. Instead, tie a piece of baling twine to one ring and bring this over the horse's head and through (but not tied) to the other ring, so that it slides freely (Fig. 31). At this stage it is important to keep the bit and the bridle disconnected, as his memory of pain is associated as much with the leather as with the steel.

He should now be opening his mouth freely for you. Place the bit in position under, but still not in, his mouth, just holding it there for a few seconds, and, before he lifts his head, take it away. This must be done several times until he accepts the presence of the bit. Now position the bit under his mouth in preparation to placing it in his mouth, then ask him to open his mouth by placing your hand (palm uppermost) under his mouth and putting your thumb inside his mouth to touch the bars. Now place the bit carefully in his open mouth. (The mouth must be sufficiently open to avoid banging his teeth as the bit is put in position.)

By placing the bit in his mouth with the twine still sliding freely through one ring of the bit, you can now manipulate the bit by pulling the twine up or letting it drop gently until the horse becomes accustomed to the bit moving around in his mouth. The war bridle must still be on, of course, and if, at any time, he lifts his head, you should apply the lightest pressure to the rope to bring his head down again. When the horse has fully accepted the introduction of the bit, take the leather headpiece and put this on, first as a separate item, followed by the bit, gradually introducing the two items together. If, at any time, the horse becomes anxious, go back a few steps to the initial handling of the head and confirm the lessons. Patience is a prime ingredient of the successful re-education of all horses.

PULLING AWAY

Another problem commonly associated with bridling is the horse that pulls away just as the bit is taken out (and therein lies the reason for the problem because the bit is taken out, as distinct from the horse being allowed to let it drop naturally from his mouth). When the bridle is removed, he gets knocked in the teeth by the bit. He has now learnt pain follows when the headpiece comes over his ears as the bridle is removed.

The cure

The approach to this situation is similar to the one described previously, in that the bit is treated as a separate unit from the headpiece. This time, however, when the bridle is put on you should leave the bit unattached to the headpiece but have the twine still connected. Place the bridle on the horse's head, keeping the bit in position with the string. Now, at the point of removing the bridle, where the problem exists, lift the headpiece up and forward over his ears, maintaining upward pressure on the string. This requires a little patience before you get a feel for it but practice makes perfect. The horse will invariably pull back as the headpiece is removed, expecting the pain associated with the bit. Keep the bit in his mouth until he lowers his head again, which he will do, then allow the bit to drop naturally by playing out the string. If he lifts his head at any time, pull up on the string again, but in such a way that the bit does not knock on his teeth.

Work in this way until the horse shows no anxiety. The headpiece can then be removed and it will now be possible to attach the bit to the bridle again. Do not hurry by rushing on to the next step before you are completely sure the first step has been totally understood and accepted. As mentioned earlier, the handler's personal confidence and liberal patience are key elements in all effective re-education procedures.

12. Weaving, cribbing and windsucking

The problem

Weaving, cribbing and windsucking are caused by boredom and from copying other horses displaying the same problems. Collectively, they are sometimes termed stable vices and are virtually unknown in horses which live in groups in an open environment.

The cure

There are no known cures for weaving, cribbing or windsucking but preventive measures can be taken and have, in the main, proved effective in reducing the problem although not the cause.

WEAVING

In weaving, the horse moves his head and neck from side to side, mostly while standing still, although some horses also lift their front legs to compensate for the shifting of weight as they rock, pendulum-like, to and fro. Stable-bound horses are found to be most prone to this condition but, to date, although irritating and unsightly to watch, it appears that no damage results from the practice. The condition can be eased by putting the horse out to graze in a large paddock for a few hours each day. If this is impractical and the horse must remain confined to stable or yard, the introduction of some toys to play with has been found to be of some benefit. Try a hanging tyre or a football or the introduction of music to the stable area. A stabled horse that weaves generally hangs his head over the top of the half door and it has been found an effective deterrent to hang cans filled with small stones at regular intervals above the opening, so that, in weaving, he bangs his head repeatedly. You could also fit a special weaving grille which does not allow the horse space to weave although he can still put his head out over the door.

CRIBBING

Cribbing is another habit formed by stabled and yarded horses. The horse takes hold of any biteable surface with his teeth and holds on to it constantly, causing damage not only to his teeth but to stalls, fences and equipment. Sump oil, creosote or similar bad-tasting substances can be painted on the surfaces bitten to act as a deterrent but they cannot provide a cure.

WINDSUCKING

Windsucking is an advanced or progressed form of cribbing. Now the horse not only cribs but opens his mouth to suck in air while biting. By filling up with air in this way he can lose condition. Because his stomach feels full, he does not eat enough food.

Aids such as windsucking collars are available and have been found to be partially effective. These are fitted tightly around the gullet of the horse so that, as he takes in air, he expands his neck muscles, putting pressure on the collar which prevents him from swallowing. (Such collars have their place but the author has seen chronic windsuckers with terrible bruises and lacerations on their necks due to constant pressure from the collar, yet still the animal persists in cribbing and attempting to windsuck.)

Small nails covered by sacking can also have a curative effect. When the horse latches on to the fence he is pricked by the nails. If he persists, longer, sharper nails can be employed.

NB: It is strongly advised that you never allow a horse known to have this habit on to your property because in a very short space of time all other horses in contact with him will copy this incurable habit.

Weaving, cribbing and windsucking

13. Biting

The problem

Biting is used as a display of aggression in some horses and is caused either by experiences of mismanagement or because he is a group1 (dominant) type in the hierarchy of horse types. A true biter is capable of taking a man in his teeth and lifting him off the ground, causing considerable pain and injury. The innocence of nipping in a foal can develop into a prime vice in the grown horse. If only for reasons of safety, all habits or responses that feature biting on the part of the horse must be stopped immediately.

The cure

The correction that the horse receives from the handler must be applied to the offending part, namely the mouth. Make the punishment short and sharp. For example, when grooming or saddling have a flathead nail ready in your hand, with the head projecting from between the third and fourth knuckles of your fist, so that he punishes himself as he swings his mouth and head into your fist. On no account take your hand to him but, rather, let him come to you.

An alternative is to lift your elbow so that it strikes him in the face as he turns to bite. The author strongly cautions against slapping the horse on the mouth with an open hand. This will only encourage him to try again and the lesson will quickly degenerate into a game. There is a considerable difference between aggression and the horse that bites another in the ritual before mating. Horses also mouth and fondle their handlers on occasions and this can safely be encouraged, without concern that it might develop as a vice.

14. Kicking

The problem

Practically all kicking problems in horses can be traced to earlier experiences of rough handling, grooming or girthing up too quickly. It is also known to result from boredom in the stable.

The cure

The war bridle can be used to great effect in stopping this highly dangerous habit. To effect a cure, the horse should be in a position where he is likely to kick – this may be when being groomed or when saddling up. Fit the horse with the war bridle, handling him with an air of confidence. At the point where he shifts weight to take his leg off the ground in order to kick, correct instantly with a sharp tug on the rope. When he puts his leg to the ground, immediately stroke his neck and tell him 'Whoa'. Go back again to grooming or saddling, insisting that he accepts the touch of your hand regardless of where you choose to place it on him and correcting him immediately he shifts weight to raise his leg.

It is important to resist any temptation to growl or shout at him; simply correct using the rope. When you have placed the saddle on his back and before you finally girth him up, he may indicate to you that he is ticklish or 'girthy' by tightening the muscles around the girth region or moving away from your touch. Placing the flat of your hand against his belly prepares him for the coldness of the girth.

Horses that turn their hindquarters on you in the yard or box and then back up to kick, must first be given a face-up lesson. Following this, take a sack filled with two or three shovel loads of sand and tie this to his tail so that it hangs down at about hock level. He will discover that kicking at the sack has no effect except to cause considerable discomfort to himself. Leaving the sack tied to him in this fashion, for perhaps three or four hours at a time, has a great curative effect and should be repeated as necessary.

Hosing also achieves the same effect. Keep the water playing on his hind legs until he accepts the sensation and stops kicking. Making a 'flag' with a soft towel and then controlling him with the war bridle if he moves away or raises his leg to kick also has the desired effect. Using the 'flag' enables you to stand clear of his legs in case he does attempt to kick but, more important, it also allows you to continue using it when he does so. Do not frighten the horse by flapping it all round him but keep it on his legs while he shows an inclination to kick, taking it off only when he stops.

15. Hard to catch

The problem

In the vast majority of cases, horses that are difficult to catch have simply learnt the benefits associated with *not* being caught and this implies mishandling and an absence of suitable training at an earlier age. During this period, it is likely that no reward was forthcoming when the horse was caught, so, by degrees, the horse came to understand that to be caught was to be worked.

It is a mistake to assume that hay or grain left in a paddock container helps in overcoming this problem. When the handler is out of sight, an unhaltered working horse will feed at its discretion and, later, when it is time to be caught, the horse will still act evasively, remembering the work but not the feed. When a horse is kept in a paddock without yard facilities, it is of great benefit to establish the habit of haltering and tying up prior to feeding. By this means, the relationship of feed and halter will become firmly bonded in the horse's memory.

Cure 1

To avoid the marathon exercise of trying to catch and the inevitable chase, first teach him the face-up lesson. Having taught this at an early age, the horse will offer himself to be caught by facing and walking to the handler, irrespective of the size of yard or paddock.

Cure 2

If time does not allow the handler to halter and tie the horse while he feeds, a yard, stall or shelter must be erected in a corner of the paddock and it is essential that the horse be fed *only* in this place. Horses are creatures of habit and are quickly conditioned to routines as long as they are adhered to *at all times.* It is essential that the horse is caught each time and, having experienced the haltering with feeding, the handler will then have an opportunity to teach the face-up lesson in the yard. This area has to become a *comfort zone.* If the routine is always carried out,

soon the horse will willingly enter the yard when he sees the handler coming. It must be pointed out again that for 100 per cent success, the horse must *only* be fed (and this includes titbits) in the yard, shelter or pen.

Cure 3

If you are unable to build a yard, pen or shelter and the horse allows himself to be caught only on occasions, this calls for the use of hobbles. Hobbles are commonly used in Australia, America and other countries where horses are grazed in large unfenced areas, but in countries where grazing is restricted to much smaller fields, hobbles may not only be considered unconventional but also unacceptable. In the UK, animal welfare organisations are opposed in principle to tethering, and hobbling is seen as a tethering method. The Protection Against Cruel Tethering Act 1988, clearly states that it is an offence to tether any horse, ass or mule under such conditions or in such a manner as to cause unnecessary suffering. However, extreme situations call for extreme methods, and if a handler has never experienced the frustration of hours, if not days, spent in trying to catch a horse in large, open tracts of land, they might find it difficult to appreciate the benefits of hobbles.

Hobbles are generally made of leather with a heavy-gauge chain between the straps and are buckled around the horse's pasterns. When introducing a pair of hobbles to the horse for the first time, they must be attached while the horse is in a confined, safe area, allowing him to become accustomed to their restrictions. Once released back into the paddock, he will still be able to move fairly easily, but at a much slower pace, thus enabling the handler to catch him.

Hobbling should only be necessary to remedy earlier mishandling. Teach the face-up lesson. Halter and reward him with affection each day and he will soon be pleading to be caught.

16. Shying

The problem

Although an instinctive behavioural response, the reaction of shying in a horse can be attributed to boredom, a general feeling of insecurity, a lack of confidence or a weak and nervous rider and can also be a habit formed in response to earlier experiences so that he always swerves to the side at an unexpected noise or moving object. The habit of shying generally occurs more commonly in Thoroughbreds and youngsters, rather than in older, more experienced and cold blooded horses.

The cure

A horse can often be corrected of shying when ridden by a strong rider who keeps him faced up to whatever he is likely to shy at. Invariably, horses prone to shying are nervous horses anyway and, having shied, the rider's instinct is to stop the horse (this is a reward) and pet him (this is a reward also). In trying to soothe the horse, you are confirming that there really is something to be scared about. Through your own actions, you have shown the horse that there is great benefit to shying. The rider has inadvertently reinforced a fear by giving rewards.

Riding a young horse out for the first time is bound to find him looking at things cautiously but with a confident rider he will soon overcome any anxiety, coming to develop a bold approach to the unknown. In the hands of a nervous rider the same animal will develop into a nervous horse, alert for anything that induces shying. Every horse must learn to trust his rider, believing that the rider will never ask him to go anywhere that would prove dangerous. In treating this problem, ignore the shying and ride forward strongly. Do not talk or try to reassure. Look somewhere else and so will he.

17. Rearing and striking

The problem

A horse that rears can be considered an extremely dangerous animal as he is capable of killing or crippling both handler or rider and, by falling backwards, may even kill himself.

The cure

Both rearing and striking can be nipped in the bud but only if caught very early in their development and before forming as a habit of response. When handling a confirmed rearer on the ground, carry a lunge or stock whip. As soon as the horse begins to go up, strike him severely across the forelegs, quitting immediately he comes down. When he has come down, ask him to come forward to you, rewarding him with your voice and a stroke of his neck. *Do not* talk to him at the point of correcting with the whip. If he persists with rearing, strike him yet again across the forelegs. The foregoing may appear to be severe treatment but a dangerous habit such as this demands positive, sharp action, and is not to be treated lightly.

REARING

No foolproof cure exists for a confirmed rearer but there are some simple safety rules that can be followed to the advantage of both horse and rider. One of these results from the observation that when the horse rears there is a strong possibility that he will also topple over backwards. It is therefore very important to let go of the rope or reins (depending on whether handling from the ground or being mounted as rider), in case you cause the horse to lose his balance. If you are riding, lean as far forward as possible, letting go of the reins completely. In the event that the horse should lose his balance and begin to fall backwards, an agile rider can quickly slip off over his hindquarters.

In some cases, a horse that has reared and fallen can be kept down on the ground by sitting on his head or neck, which effectively denies him the ability to get up. He will find this demoralising and this strategy has been known to be of some effect in stopping rearing but the author hastens to add that such tactics are not for the inexperienced rider or handler. The practice of hitting a horse, at the point of rearing, with a piece of four by two (wood), a whip, a bag of water, etc., will achieve nothing in attempting a cure for rearing but will undoubtably increase the psychological damage to the horse.

Worth consideration is the fact that, to rear, a horse must be at a standstill and, quite often, it can be observed that horses become agitated by having to stand still. As a good example, ex-race horses often display this symptom, having been trained all of their working lives to go forward energetically. Being asked to stand still induces anxiety in the horse and when a rider then continually niggles at the bit, the horse cannot do anything else but go up. The exercise of turning him in a tiny circle or of doubling him back on himself can often be of help in preventing rearing. Also of help is the practice of keeping him walking in a circle until you are ready to move off. It must be stressed, however, that these are preventive measures only – there is no known cure for rearing.

Many seasoned horsemen offer the view that the only real cure for a persistent rearer is a piece of lead between the horse's eyes.

STRIKING

Striking may develop as a horse pulls back on a lead rope and rears when being led by a handler. This is usually seen in a horse with an aggressive nature that may hide other problems. Striking will, eventually, develop into rearing if the horse is allowed to find a positive outlet for this aggression. The methods described as a cure for rearing may also be used with confidence as a means to stop the striker. Another method is to place hobbles on the forelegs of the horse, which are secured above the knees. This, in effect, limits the movement of the front legs at the moment of striking.

18. Bucking

The problem

The habit of bucking in a horse broken to saddle is an unacceptable vice and should not be allowed. A horse that has been backed (broken in) correctly will not buck with the rider on board. In fact, the horse does not buck initially in order to get rid of the rider but, under the right circumstances, it can learn that to buck holds all the benefits of a reward. A case in point might be to imagine a young rider mounted on a pony. It is spring and the animal is full of the joys of that season so he puts in a little hump or pigroot and, unintentionally, dislodges the child who falls roughly to the ground.

This creates a great deal of insecurity in the child who now has little enthusiasm for remounting. The pony gets scolded and is returned to his box, yard or paddock (a nice reward for kicking up one's heels!). A few days later he bucks again and, what do you know – back in the yard! By this random sequence of events, the pony has learnt that to dislodge the weight on his back is to be rewarded by returning to the yard or box for a rest.

The cure

There are several ways to cure bucking and we shall discuss three of the more common ones here. One favourite way among many professional trainers is to lead the horse, fully saddled, to a very steep hill and, having mounted, push him forward with strong aids. Simply by using their legs, a practised rider can prompt a horse into bucking. The rider forces the horse up the hill. The horse will try bucking for a few strides but, finding it very hard work, the bucking will stop. This method also works well when used in conjunction with the next method.

Put the horse into a round yard or pen and tie up the off foreleg. Saddle him but, before mounting, encourage him forward on three legs into canter. The seasoned bucker will even try bucking on three legs but will quit trying fairly quickly. Now mount and encourage him forward. It will be found that, after some initial attempts at bucking, he will begin to go forward quite nicely. Any horse that is moving forward with energy is less likely to buck so it is an advantage to have the horse listen to the aids and keep him moving forward, the point here being that he must slow down to buck.

Yet a third method, when you feel him raise his back just prior to bucking, is to turn him abruptly. This is because this action, when effected quickly, succeeds in momentarily unbalancing the horse both mentally and physically. To make this turn, slide your hand down one rein (either side will do) and, having taken up the slack, turn him so that his head comes very sharply around to his quarters. Then send him forward immediately in the direction of his head.

19. Bolting

The problem

It is not clearly understood what triggers the action of bolting in a horse but it is known to occur even in the most docile of breeds and for no apparent cause. Bolting can therefore be said to result from panic induced by unknown fears. A characteristic of the bolting horse is that his senses shut down – he sees, hears and feels nothing. As these traits become evident, the rider is faced with the almost impossible task of gaining the horse's attention sufficiently to steer and slow him down. There are no foolproof cures for a horse that bolts, but some specific education can significantly lessen the potential for it to occur.

Before riding forward for the first time on an unknown horse, the practised rider always takes the precaution of checking that he has adequate 'brakes' and 'steering'. This is done at the walk, before proceeding to trot and canter. If, during this process, it is discovered that there is a tendency in the horse to 'lean' or 'lumberneck' (that is, having requested the horse to turn to a light feel on the rein, he turns his head only and continues in a straight line), work him through 'yielding to the rein'. This lesson is accomplished by working the horse on the ground and tying his head to his tail for ten minutes on each side, thus teaching him to 'follow' his head.

Having completed this lesson successfully, saddle and mount the horse and proceed to request, through the rein aid, that he turn his head to both sides.

The next step is to teach him to 'double'. This is done by riding the horse at trot parallel to, and approximately 2 m (6½ ft) from, the fence line of the arena. (Do not attempt this lesson in an open paddock.) Riding anticlockwise, trot energetically for four or five strides down the fence line, then slide your right hand halfway down the rein, still maintaining contact with the horse's mouth. At the same time, allow your weight to come down into the saddle, turning your upper body towards the fence to look in the new direction, which will have the effect of encouraging the horse to turn. Use a strong outside leg (in this instance, it will be your left), as the turn must be executed quickly. As soon as the horse slows down and has turned his head, kick him into a brisk trot in the new direction. Repeat regularly on both reins and you will find that he soon begins responding to your body position as you allow your weight to drop in the saddle in preparation for the turn. When he is responding quickly and willingly, progress to the canter.

This is also a particularly good lesson for any young horse that has been freshly backed (broken to saddle), as it immediately displays your control to him.

This lesson must also be performed in an enclosed arena, and one that has a good and consistent surface.

Saddle and mount the horse, putting him into canter on a large circle. Maintain a very light contact, allowing him to move forward. When he increases his speed, do *not* attempt to slow him with the reins. Riding on the right rein (clockwise), move your right (inside) hand away from the horse and towards the centre of the circle, maintaining a fairly loose rein. Give directional tugs with the right rein only to keep him on line. The left (outside) rein must remain passive. The circle should be no more than 20 m in diameter, which will allow you to keep him moving forward at the canter, maintaining the 'open' effect of your right hand. Make absolutely no attempt to slow him with either rein but do not allow *him* to slow either. It has to become *your* decision (as far as he understands), to stay in the forward-moving canter.

After five minutes of cantering, he may be looking to slow down. Put your weight in the saddle in preparation for stopping and allow him to slow down a little. Then immediately lift your weight slightly and, staying very relaxed in the saddle, push him on once again into a forward-moving canter. The important element in the exercise is that the selection of the pace becomes *your* decision. Persist with the cantering until you can slow the horse at will, then push him on again. This may take up to 30

minutes or more. When he begins to show obvious signs of tiredness, push him on again, stopping him *only* when he is quite fatigued.

Having made your decision to stop, tug him into an ever-decreasing circle with the right (inside) rein, but do not use your legs at all. Because of the size of the circle he will reach the point where he cannot canter any more, so keep turning him until he trots then walks and eventually stops. Keep tugging at the right rein, even when he has stopped, to keep his head 'snugged' around. Now, using the left rein, coax his head to the front with gentle tugging. Walk him forward on a long rein for a few minutes, then repeat the whole exercise once again in the opposite direction.

Work the horse in this manner for a period of one week and he will soon be looking to stop at the slightest indication from the rider, having learnt from the previous experience the unpleasantness of pressured work. This teaches the horse that you are in total control over his actions.

If, having worked the horse in the above situations, he still persists in running away with the rider, the author suggests that you 'bale out', allowing the horse go on alone to his grave after the inevitable accident, or treat him to an early demise before he ends a human life.

Notes on buying

I very much hope that one of the benefits of having read this book from cover to cover will be that the reader now has sufficient knowledge to select a horse for purchase with some confidence.

BEWARE THE DRUGGED HORSE

Unfortunately, the horse market still harbours many dealers or owners who resort to the use of drugs to conceal any number of faults and vices when selling a horse to an unsuspecting buyer. It could be the next horse you buy!

Drugs are used to quieten the nervous and erratic horse, reduce a swelling on a leg and to cover up lameness, giving the illusion of a sound animal. Drugs have been known to anaesthetise a fracture in the leg of a horse for up to an hour, with a view to selling. In some instances, studying the eye can detect whether a drug has been used. The eye of a drugged horse takes on a 'sleepy' appearance and a greyish tone can be observed.

OTHER POINTS WORTH CHECKING

Apart from watching out for the use of drugs as a means to conceal an unsoundness, certain other aspects of the horse are equally as important to assess. Some of these can make the horse unfit for the purpose for which you are purchasing him.

There follows a brief guide to the main areas of concern when looking at a horse with a view to purchase. It is *always* well worth paying for a thorough check by a veterinary surgeon. One should also be cautious about the opinions of friends, no matter how well intentioned.

DEFECTS OF THE EYE

Because of the unique structure and location of the horse's eye, any defect found here is said to be an unsoundness. Loss of sight due to cataract (recognised as opaque) or blindness is an obvious fault and may, at times, cause the horse to shy.

ROARING, WHISTLING AND BROKEN WIND

All of these can be heard after the horse undergoes extreme exertion. 'High blowing' can be heard when the horse shows excitement or exuberance, generally disappearing when he has settled down. Grunting is also heard at times as a horse exerts energy at the point of jumping an obstacle and on landing but this is not considered an unsoundness, simply a noise created by power and energy.

ACTION OF THE LIMBS

Any lameness is an unsoundness. Conformation faults, such as dishing and paddling (swinging the forelegs in an inward or outward arc respectively), are unsightly but the horse is not considered unsound by their presence unless the second of the two is creating a lameness.

By trotting the horse away from and back to the buyer, it will be possible to detect such defects.

DISEASE

Any sign of disease that affects the heart, digestion, respiratory system, skin, feet or urinary organs constitutes an unsoundness. Your veterinary surgeon will locate any fault in these areas.

BLEMISH

Although unsightly, blemishes such as scars and firing marks (uncommon these days) are acceptable and not considered an unsoundness. A splint will also be unsightly but need not be considered an unsoundness unless next to, or interfering with, the joint of the leg.

CONFORMATION

In truth, the best 'put-together' horse may not necessarily prove to be the top performance horse. Depending on your chosen sport, the ideal conformation will vary considerably.

TEETH

Ageing the horse at the point of purchase is very important and must be done with a degree of accuracy. A horse is said to have a 'full mouth' at five years of age. He is known to be 'aged' at eight years and over. If a horse has had a relatively easy life, he will still be quite useful as a hack at 15 years and onwards but, given a life of strenuous work, the same horse will be considered fit only for pasture.

Caveat emptor! (let the buyer beware!)

A thorough veterinary check should reveal not only limb and wind soundness but also, from blood and urine tests taken, the true state of the horse's well-being, and is a wise investment before parting with your money.

Glossary
of terms

Throughout this book, various terms are used to describe specific procedures or conditions encountered in horse handling. The following glossary of terms is offered as a helpful guide in defining the meaning of each and the context in which it is used when encountered in the text.

COMFORT ZONE

Any area, nominated by the handler, that must be discovered and occupied by the horse to achieve a sense of confidence and security.

CORRECTING

Pressure applied in various ways through use of the war bridle, which encourages the horse to take up any position nominated by the handler.

FACE-UP

The horse's focused attention while he awaits the handler's next request. This requires that he face the handler straight on with his body turned to neither left nor right.

FOLLOWING

The horse accompanies the handler without hesitation, on a slack rope or rein, following wherever the handler chooses to go.

REWARD

A comfortable and unrestrained condition that is experienced by the horse, immediately following the application of a more or less constant pressure applied through the rope by the handler.

SLACK

Without tension or pressure in the rope extending between horse and handler.

STRETCH THE ROPE

The handler has placed their weight in their hip, the horse leans back, his weight shifted to his hindquarters. The rope therefore has no slack but a small amount of tension. The handler maintains this tension, the horse leans back, stretching the rope, and is induced to come forward.

TUGGING

The precise action of exerting a rapid tug only, upon a rope void of slack, and then releasing the pressure instantly. Distinct from an incorrect and prolonged 'pulling' action.

WEIGHT IN HIP

Positioning one's own body to counteract force. Achieved by placing one's weight off centre. Leaning back and favouring one leg over the other, so that the body weight seems to be focused in that hip (similar to a tug-o-war posture).

AREA OR YARD

Alternative terms used in Britain and Australia to describe a confined area.

JAN MAY

In conclusion

For a good many years I have been involved in the handling and training of horses and, having gone the distance, find myself pondering frequently over the enormous variety of personalities and characters that have come before me in the shape of the horse. I have come to the conclusion that, no matter how long one is involved in the horse world, in some way the horse will, to a large extent, remain a mystery. He offers a refinement in his acceptance of us, while still remaining aloof to a certain degree, and it is this part of him that will always remain a separate and private affair.

Sadly, in the vast range of character traits and personalities that make up various individuals who work with horses, there still remains the 'average' handler who delivers to the horse a training method that involves fear and pain combined with abuse and ignorance, and who will never know the obedience and trust that the horse has to offer.

JAN MAY